# James
# STEWART

# *James* STEWART

## Helene McGowan

**Crescent Books**

**New York**

This 1992 edition published by Crescent
Books,
distributed by Outlet Book Company, Inc.,
a Random House Company,
225 Park Avenue South,
New York, New York 10003

Produced by
Brompton Books Corporation
15 Sherwood Place
Greenwich, CT 06830

ISBN 0-517-06708-0

8 7 6 5 4 3 2 1

Printed and bound in Hong Kong

*Page 1:* A publicity shot of James Stewart taken in
1939.

*Page 2:* Stewart in one of his last westerns, *Shenandoah*
(1965).

*Right:* James Stewart playing one of his most famous
roles, the legendary bandleader Glenn Miller, whom
he portrayed in *The Glenn Miller Story* (1954).

*Opposite:* Stewart looks as though he means business
as Glyn McLyntock in *Bend of the River* (1952), which
some regard as the finest of the five Mann/Stewart
westerns of the 1950s.

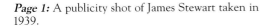

# Contents

# Chapter 1
# THE MAKING OF A STAR
# *1908-1935*

INDIANA, Pennsylvania, where James Stewart was born on May 20, 1908, is just the kind of patriotic, friendly, country town that featured in so many of his most popular films. James Maitland Stewart was the first child of Alex and Elizabeth Stewart, who ran the local hardware store, J M Stewart and Sons. Jimmy was named after his paternal grandfather who founded the store in 1853. A sister, Mary, arrived four years after Jimmy in 1912 and Virginia, the third and last child, was born in 1914.

Indiana was a small town with a population of approximately 6000 when Stewart was born. Set in the rolling hills of the Allegheny mountains, only an hour's drive from Pittsburg, the town was an economically diverse community with interests in farming, mining and rubber factories. Indiana even boasted a university, IUP (Indiana University of Pennsylvania), founded in 1875 and occupying over a hundred acres today. Stewart's affection for his home town has not diminished; he believes the town is 'the way all America should be.' He has certainly always remained true to the old-fashioned spirit of his birthplace. The extravagances and excesses of Hollywood made little sense to Stewart: 'I am a Presbyterian. I support the Salvation Army and the Boy Scouts. They are considered quaint in some quarters but I admire their work. I've become known as a Republican. I have always been a Conservative and I come from a Conservative background.'

When Anthony Quayle directed James Stewart in the British production of the popular play *Harvey* in London in 1975, he said of the star: 'Jimmy is everything the British audience wants an American to be but so rarely is.' It is Indiana that helped to make Stewart that kind of American: an honest, courteous, humorous, gentle, determined

*Left:* The two-year-old Jimmy calmly holds the camera's gaze as he rides his tricycle in his hometown of Indiana, Pennsylvania. Jimmy was fortunate enough to inherit his mother's steady temperament and good looks.

man. He grew up influenced by the town's sense of values, most particularly a belief in the importance of community, the family, the church and hard work. It has sometimes been said that Stewart excelled in playing different versions of himself and there is some truth in that observation, but it is also a gross oversimplification of Stewart's art given that he has played a surprisingly wide variety of roles – gunfighters, journalists, lawyers, and college professors to name a few. He has appeared in everything from westerns and sophisticated, light comedies to tense psycho-dramas. But James Stewart will be remembered above all for his embodiment of America's idealized sense of itself. His greatest strength has been his unique ability to characterize what is best in American life; he has reflected his country's

faith that the honorable, incorruptible, moral citizen still exists in ordinary, small-town American life, small towns just like James Stewart's Indiana.

The young Jimmy enjoyed a Tom Sawyer childhood in the Stewart's comfortable, spacious house on a steep hillside overlooking the town. His mother Elizabeth was a calm, dignified woman who was very active in Indiana's Ladies Guild. She was a devout churchgoer and played the organ in the church choir. Alex Stewart, Jimmy's father, was a different character altogether, a veteran of the Spanish American and First World Wars. He was 46 when he enlisted in the army to fight the Kaiser and was posted to Camp Dodge in Iowa where he served as a captain. Jimmy's grandfather on his father's side served with the

Union army in the Civil War. Alex and Jimmy were very close; Elizabeth Stewart once told a reporter that you could pay Jimmy no greater compliment than to tell him he reminded you of his father. Alex was a believer in plain living and blunt speaking and passed on to his son his distaste for 'high falutin' living.'

The Stewart's hardware store was a focus of community life in Indiana. J M Stewart and Sons was no ordinary store; it was sometimes closer to a museum thanks to Alex's soft heart and disinclination to refuse any items offered him in lieu of cash. The place was cluttered with interesting but useless items such as a German helmet, silver loving cups, and a music box that played the last aria from *Madam Butterfly*. Most exotic of all was the twelve-foot python that a traveling side show once gave to Alex in exchange for a hacksaw, a glass cutter and a toilet brush, rather more practical items. Jimmy was quite happy to feed this monster with mice caught in the basement, but one day an elderly spinster witnessed the grisly ritual (the snake resided in the shop's front window) and sued Alex for 'endangering her life and limb.' The suit was dropped when Alex agreed to get rid of the snake, which was chloroformed and transported to a local zoo. It was only when the usually placid Elizabeth put her foot down with the admonition 'Stop! You

already have enough junk to open your own yard!' that Alex reluctantly turned down a suit of Spanish armor. Abraham Jarvis, an Indiana local, remembers the store as a 'warmhearted place, a kind of credit heaven'.

Unsurprisingly, Stewart's earliest memories are the sights and sounds of his parents' store. Alex cherished long-held hopes that Jimmy would take over the old place when he, Stewart senior, retired; he was still waiting and hoping when he died at 89. Jimmy was the most patriotic boy in town. When Alex enlisted during the First World War, Jimmy pleaded for a copy of his father's uniform to be made for him. He wrote two anti-German plays, *The Slacker* and *To Hell with the Kaiser*, and performed them in the cellar.

Jimmy had a good time at school where he was much better at science subjects than the three 'Rs.' He was clever at engineering ways to lessen his domestic workload. When his father set him the task of weeding the large garden, Jimmy remembered the clever trick dreamed up by the real Tom Sawyer and turned the task into a competition for his friends; the boy who collected the most weeds would be declared 'weed champion of the world.' The Stewart garden and vegetable patch was soon weed free. Jimmy's desire to construct a crystal radio set was a much more

difficult challenge but he eventually mastered it when he was eleven years old.

Jimmy's good performance in the sciences at school led to his parents giving him a chemistry set for Christmas one year. The young scientist decided to make a stink bomb, which was so successful it stank out the whole house. Desperate to escape the dreadful stench, Jimmy asked if he could sleep on the front porch but his mother had thought up the perfect punishment and he was made to sleep in his bedroom where he had manufactured the bomb. Another amusing misadventure came when Jimmy put on a magic show with his friend Billy Naff. The two boys gathered a paying audience to watch them perform. The main event was to be the sawing in half of Mary Stewart, Jimmy's seven-year-old sister (a trick lifted from the pages of Jimmy's book on magic). As soon as she saw the blade, Mary very sensibly screamed and ran. Jimmy failed to appease the disgruntled audience with his accordion playing.

Stewart has two especially precious memories of his youth in Indiana and both involve major historical events from way outside small-town American life. He was recuperating at home after a bout of scarlet fever when, on his 19th birthday, May 20, 1927, Charles A. Lindbergh made his famous Lone Eagle flight

*Below:* Stewart played his boyhood hero in the 1957 *The Spirit of St Louis*, a much cherished project which recreated Charles Lindbergh's historic 1927 solo transatlantic flight to Paris. Sadly, the film was a huge financial flop. Here Stewart is seen chatting to Mrs Blanche Stuart Scott, one of the female aviation pioneers, during the making of the film.

from New York to Paris. All of Indiana went wild with excitement when Lindbergh's plane landed in Paris; 'It was just like New Year's Eve' is how Jimmy remembers it, and he built a model of Lindbergh's plane *The Spirit of St Louis*. This was not his first introduction to planes and flying, however, as he had had his first flying lesson when he was only eleven – a fifteen-minute ride for ten dollars. He grew to love flying, a private pleasure which became very important to him. He considered taking it up as a profession and has claimed: 'If I hadn't gone to Hollywood, I'm sure I would have become a flyer.'

Another treasured memory twins the intensely personal with the larger forces of history. President Warren G Harding died on August 2, 1923 and a few days later, his funeral train passed through a town a few miles from Indiana on its way to the president's home. Jimmy was there to witness this event, although his mother had initially forbidden him to go as the train was scheduled to run through at 3.30 am. One can imagine his delight when his father woke him at 2.30 am on the all-important morning with the whisper: 'Jim, boy, get up. It's time to go and see the funeral train.' Together they sneaked out of the house and arrived just in time to see the train through. At his father's behest, the fifteen-year-old Jimmy placed two pennies on the rail tracks so the train could mark them as it rolled over them. 'For years,' Jimmy later recalled, 'Dad and I carried those pennies flattened by the weight of history. And the knowledge that what was in my pocket was also in his made me feel very close to him and close to Indiana.'

One can easily understand why Stewart looks back on his childhood years with such fondness:

When I was eight we moved to Vinegar Hill, a rambling house of no particular architecture but with a large front porch loaded with wicker furniture. The living room, high ceilinged and trimmed with dark woodwork, held a grand piano, around which we gathered for family sings. My sister Virginia played the piano, my oldest sister, Mary, played violin, and I played the accordion – after a fashion. During these sessions Dad sang very softly – compared to the bellowing he did in Church – so as not to cover up Mother's clear sweet voice. Her name was Elizabeth and he called her Bessie and adored her. Though small and gentle, and not given to contention, she frequently had her way over his because she possessed patience and endurance.

When he finished ninth grade, Jimmy was sent away to boarding school at Mercersburg Academy in Pennsylvania. This was a private institution with an excellent reputation; Jimmy was lucky to get in as his year was oversubscribed but Alex Stewart would not take no

**Left:** Flying was a much loved hobby of Stewart's for many years. He made his first flight at 11 years old – $10 for a 15-minute ride. During the Second World War he served his country with honor when he joined the US Air Force in 1941. By the time he was discharged in 1945 he had attained the rank of Colonel. He went on to serve in the US Air Force Reserve and is seen here as Brigadier General James Stewart in 1968, the year he retired after 27 years of military service.

for an answer. Jimmy enjoyed his time at the school, where he was a popular figure involved in most activities. He became captain of the lightweight football team and excelled as a high hurdler and high jumper. He was art director of the school yearbook, for which he also drew cartoons, and sang and played accordion in the school choir. He returned home to Indiana every summer and would easily slip back into his family's routine and help in his father's store. Addie Ross was a next-door neighbor of the Stewarts who remembered Jimmy as:

The most steadfast boy I've ever known, as well as being the most unpretentious. He must have gotten his modesty from his mother, Alex certainly didn't have any to spare.

What Alex did have plenty of was ambition for his only son. His major objective was that Jimmy should follow him to Princeton, where the young Alex had been something of a legend. His escapades were many but the most famous was the occasion when he and some of his friends carried a cow to the top of Princeton's Nassau Hall. The reasoning behind the prank was that, with the benefit of a college education, the cow was 'sure to give better milk.'

Jimmy decided to major in civil engineering when he arrived at Princeton in the fall of 1928 but soon recognized he had made a mistake and switched to architecture. His decision was helped along by the forthrightness of one of his professors who informed him: 'Stewart, you do not have the slightest aptitude for engineering! I strongly suggest that you try something else!' The new choice of subject suited Jimmy far better and his grades improved to above average.

Much more important to the future life and career of James Stewart, Hollywood legend, was his decision to join the university's Triangle Club, the dramatics society that included the future director Joshua Logan among its members. It was in a play written by Logan that Jimmy made his first theatrical appearance. He played the part of a young accordion player in a musical and sang a song called 'Blue Hill.' The next year (1929) saw him take the lead in *The Tiger Smiles*, singing along with Logan who wrote the operetta. In Stewart's senior year a young actress called Margaret Sullavan came to Princeton to appear as a guest in the Triangle Club's Commencement Play. She had been in the University Players, a summer stock company in West Falmouth, Massachusets with Logan. Sullavan played in *The Artist and the Lady*, with Jimmy acting as stage manager. She was the first of Jimmy's theatrical friends to make it in Hollywood and remained a useful, loyal friend to him.

Stewart gained his BSc degree in 1932 and applied for a scholarship for an MSc degree. The Great Depression had begun and architectural work was hard to come by so, at the invitation of his friend Logan, Stewart decided to spend the summer with the University Players in West Falmouth. He was taken on as an accordion player in the Old Silver Beach tea room next door to the theater but the world of film acting was not to be deprived of one of its finest exponents: 'I was the worst accordion player,' Stewart would later recall, 'I just emptied that tearoom – they were glad to get rid of me.' The University Players were already a talented bunch when Stewart joined their ranks in 1932; the group included Joshua Logan, Henry Fonda (who was married briefly to fellow player Margaret Sullavan), Mildred Natwick and many others who went on to greater recognition. In June 1932, Stewart had a small walk-on part in their opening production, a play titled *Magnolia*, written by Tarkington Booth. He was directed by Logan who thought he was 'howlingly funny in it as a lanky Southern slob.' Logan was convinced his friend should take up acting professionally

*Below:* Three generations of Stewarts are pictured together in 1930 during a break from Jimmy's studies at Princeton. From the left: Jimmy's father Alex, his grandfather James and the young student himself. They are standing in front of the J M Stewart & Sons hardware store that Grandpa Stewart founded in Indiana, Pennsylvania in 1853.

**Left:** Stewart the young Broadway hopeful is pictured with his friend Myron McCormick on stage in *Yellow Jack*, which played at the Martin Beck Theater in New York during the spring of 1934.

because Stewart 'proved to be a fine actor, honest and talented.' More parts followed in *It's a Wise Child* and *Goodbye Again*.

When Stewart heard he had been accepted for a Princeton scholarship he had to make a major decision. He was worried that his parents would have to pay for his upkeep for another year but still felt unsure about acting as a career, considering it 'no job for a man.' But he could not turn down an offer to act on Broadway in the University Players' production of *Carrie Nation*. After all, if things did not work out he could always go home and work in J M Stewart and Sons. In later years, Stewart looked back on his time with the University Players and his hesitancy about entering the acting profession:

I didn't have the remotest idea that I was going to become a professional actor. I suppose I was just swept up in a crowd that was starting out in the theater and having a lot of fun.

October 29, 1932 saw Stewart swept all the way to Broadway when he made his debut in *Carrie Nation*. The play received poor notices and ran for only 31 performances. The same producer, Arthur J Beckhard, then decided to

try his luck with another Players' production, *Goodbye Again*. This opened at the Masque Theater on Broadway on December 28, 1932, with Stewart repeating his role of the chauffeur. He had three lines and three minutes on stage but was not complaining at thirty five dollars a week and over two hundred performances. The acting business was beginning to look like a good idea, although Alex Stewart did not share this view. He regarded the idea of his son becoming an actor with the deepest suspicion, and could not understand why Jimmy was giving up the security of J M Stewart and Sons. He did, however, have a wry comment to make when Jimmy's fame and fortune led to his appointment to the Board of Trustees at Alex's beloved Princeton: '. . . maybe this acting business isn't so bad after all.'

The next few months were lean ones for Stewart, who only managed to get a few bit parts and a job as a stage manager and saw his savings rapidly diminishing. He moved into an apartment on West 63rd Street near Central Park West with his best friend Henry Fonda. The seven-story building was also home to prostitutes, who happily plied their trade all day long. As Stewart remembers: 'It was impossible to leave our apartment without stumbling on a satisfied customer.' Joshua Logan and Burgess Meredith were among those who from time to time shared the communal flat, which was pretty dismal; it had a livingroom with two battered studio couches, a bathroom, a huge kitchen stove which sat in the hallway and that was about it. Joshua Logan liked to recall the good times he had in the shared apartment:

We drank, laughed, listened to good jazz, and rotated the sleeping arrangements so as to leave the livingroom couch free for those who had dates.

During a lull in their theatrical endeavors, Stewart and his pals formed the Thursday Night Club, where they played poker and sang songs to cheer themselves up. One of its mem-

bers, the actor Myron McCormick, joked shortly before his death, 'I think he (Stewart) still owes me $3 million.'

In the early summer of 1933 Stewart was hired by a company that played in the Long Island Barn Theater; he appeared as a deranged airplane pilot. For the 1933-34 season he returned temporarily to stage managing, working for a touring company who hired him to look after their star, Miss Jane Campion, a grand actress of the old school. But Stewart's run of luck did not last and Miss Campion had him fired for spoiling her deathbed scene during a performance of *Camille* in Boston. Part of Stewart's job was to bring down the curtain and one night he was alarmed to hear two drunks squabbling in the alley outside the theater. He went outside to scare them away, and when he rushed back in again mistakenly thought he had missed his

*Right:* Another publicity shot when Stewart was just one of MGM's young male contract players. This was taken to publicize the film *Once There Was a Lady*, in which Stewart did not in the end appear.

**Left:** James Stewart and Henry Fonda play two struggling musicians, Slim and Hank, in the 1948 comedy *On Our Merry Way*. The film did poorly at the box office, and regrettably Stewart and Fonda had to wait until 1970 to make their only other film together – the comedy western *The Cheyenne Social Club*, directed by Gene Kelly.

cue and brought down the curtain. Unfortunately Miss Campion had not quite finished expiring on stage. She quickly rose from the dead to scream at Stewart: 'You've completely ruined my performance, ruined it completely!'

Happily, Broadway soon beckoned again and Stewart was offered his most important role to date, the idealistic young guinea-pig soldier in *Yellow Jack*, a dramatization of Walter Reed's fight against yellow fever in turn-of-the-century Cuba. The role involved playing an Irishman and Stewart impressed the producers with his rendition of an Irish accent; he had listened to as many Irishmen as he could find in New York. The play opened at the Martin Beck Theater on March 6, 1934 and played for several months. Stewart was praised by many of the critics and particularly impressed the reviewer for *The New York Times* who wrote: 'James Stewart seems to have talent as well as scruples . . . the play deserves a long run.' His performance secured him more than good notices; it led to a role in *Divided by Three* which starred Judith Anderson. Henry Fonda much admired his friend's performance and the memory of it stayed with him:

He was playing the son of Judith Anderson, a formidable actress. But he was standing there, eye to eye with her and he was just marvelous. In his dressingroom I looked at him and sat there shaking my head, wondering 'Where did this come from? How did he get to be so good . . .' Here was I busting my shoe leather trying to make it in the theater and here was this lackadaisical fellow Stewart just stumbling in to it.

Fonda and Stewart remained great friends throughout their years of mutual stardom, and Stewart thought just as highly of Fonda's talent. Before Stewart's big break in *Yellow Jack*, he and Fonda appeared together in a Broadway flop, *All Good Americans*. After the last night party in early 1934, the two friends were walking home across Times Square when Fonda dared Stewart to have a go at busking with his accordion. Stewart launched into his repertoire and had collected 36 cents and a small but appreciative crowd when an annoyed policeman broke up the party, rebuking them for disturbing the peace at 4.00 am.

One of Stewart's co-stars in *Divided by Three* was Hedda Hopper, later the infamous Hollywood gossip supremo. She always liked to claim responsibility for introducing Stewart to movie stardom. In her version, Hopper recommended the young actor to MGM, where she had been working as an actress and studio aide. A screen test was arranged in New York for Stewart but initially nothing came of it. The theater offers were still coming in, however, and Stewart's next Broadway appearance was in the George Abbot production of *Page Miss Glory*, which opened on November 27, 1934 and ran for 64 performances. In March 1935 Henry Fonda went to Hollywood to star in the movie version of his hit Broadway play *The Farmer Takes a Wife*. In April 1935 Stewart opened in what was to be his last stage appearance for many years, *Journey by Night*. It was a flop, which featured Stewart in the unlikely role of a Viennese bank clerk; one critic commented that Stewart was 'as Viennese as a hamburger.' But this unenthusiastic reception didn't matter for a very welcome telegram had arrived from Billy Grundy, a talent scout (and later studio executive) at MGM, who had spotted Stewart in a couple of Broadway plays. The telegram read: 'Report to Hollywood – part available with three months option on your services.' The door was open.

# Chapter 2
# THE MGM YEARS
# *1935-1938*

**Right:** A studio portrait released to publicize *The Gorgeous Hussy* (1936).

**Below:** The MGM publicity machine was always busy. This shot of Stewart playing tennis was churned out in March 1936.

WHEN James Stewart arrived in Hollywood by train, on June 8, 1935, he carried a black case containing a model airplane. It was a present for Henry Fonda, a copy of a Martin bomber that the two of them had made in the Madison Square hotel room they shared when the lease had run out on their Central Park West apartment. Billy Grundy had great faith in his latest discovery,

a faith not entirely shared by everyone at MGM. Stewart credits Grundy with getting his career off the ground: 'It was really his faith in me that got me started.' He moved in with Fonda, who helped him get used to the strange ways of Hollywood. Stewart later recalled his first impression of the movie capital:

When I arrived in Hollywood it was just as exciting as one hears. The big studios were much more than the huge factories they are today. They were big families of contract players and technicians where actors could learn their business in the best possible way – by experience.

Stewart signed a minimum wage contract with MGM; this paid him $350 a week and ran for seven years, with a renewable option every six months. The studio understandably decided that the young Stewart needed fattening up; at six foot three inches tall and 130lb, he was thought much too skinny to attract the ladies on the big screen. Stewart presented himself to the studio in-house body builder who pronounced him 'beyond help,' but Stewart worked out four days a week and forced down plenty of banana splits topped with whipped cream and dozens of thick milk shakes. Henry Fonda had also been ordered to pile on a few pounds. He let Stewart in on his calorific secret – brandy alexanders (brandy and cream shakes). Gradually they added more and more brandy to their concoctions and were often mildly and happily inebriated by 8.00 am, time for work in the studio. Before long Stewart had gained enough weight to satisfy his bosses.

Henry Rapf, a studio producer, was put in charge of Stewart's career. He put Stewart in his first film, a Spencer Tracy vehicle called

*Left:* Stewart and co-star Spencer Tracy in the Second World War drama *Malaya* (1949). Tracy had been the star of Stewart's first movie *The Murder Man* in 1935 and had picked up on Jimmy's star quality right away: 'I told him to forget the camera was there. That was all he needed. In his first scene he showed he had all the good things.'

*Below:* Stewart brought in by Nelson Eddy as a Mountie in *Rose Marie* (1936).

*The Murder Man.* Stewart played Tracy's reporter pal, nicknamed Shorty. Rapf was heard to remark: 'I should have had my head examined for giving him that part. I needed a midget, so what do they give me? A human giraffe!' Spencer Tracy was kind to the newcomer and impressed by him: 'I told him to forget the camera was there,' he once explained. 'That was all he needed. In his first scene he showed he had all the good things.' But Stewart felt he looked very gauche on screen and wondered if he should have stuck to architecture. It is hard to imagine Stewart playing the role of a Chinaman, but he did once test for such a part. He was convinced he looked the part when all made up for it but, walking around the studio lot, he was greeted with the usual 'Hello Jimmy' from everyone who knew him. The role (in *The Good Earth*) eventually went to a five foot two inch Chinese actor.

Stewart's second film appearance was in *Rose Marie* (1936) with Jeanette MacDonald and Nelson Eddy. The role of MacDonald's weak, spoilt, younger brother who turns to crime and is arrested by Eddy's Canadian Royal Mountie is a small one but it got Stewart noticed by the critics, one of whom wrote: 'I think you will like him. The Mounties are not the only people who will be out to get this man.' Margaret Sullavan was now a big star at

Universal. At her insistence, Stewart was tested and then cast in her next picture, *Next Time We Love*. Edward H Griffith directed this 'woman's picture' in which Stewart and Sullavan play man and wife, an ambitious reporter and a struggling young actress. Their careers come between them but all is well by the end of the picture – allowing for the fact that the Stewart character has contracted a fatal disease while working in China. The film did not do too well but was a good choice for Stewart. As was to happen throughout his career, the reviewers were kind to him; one called his performance 'natural, spontaneous and altogether excellent.'

In his next film, *Wife Versus Secretary*, Stewart shared the screen with three of Hollywood's biggest names – Clark Gable, Jean Harlow and Myrna Loy. The two women vie for Gable's attentions in the story (it's not difficult to guess which one played the wife), and Stewart plays the boyfriend who innocently gets caught between them. The fledgling movie star found his kissing scenes with 'the blonde bombshell' very enjoyable: 'That Jean Harlow sure was a good kisser. I realized after that that I had never really been kissed . . . Well, I forgot my lines that's what I did.' Stewart's career was progressing nicely and as far as the critics were concerned he could do no

*Below:* Stewart was lucky enough to appear with Myrna Loy, Clark Gable and Jean Harlow (with whom he is pictured) in only his third film *Wife Versus Secretary* in 1936. The 'blonde bombshell' quite blew his mind in their kissing scenes.

*Opposite:* Stewart and Joan Crawford in a scene from the silly period melodrama *The Gorgeous Hussy*. Described as 'fiction founded upon historical fact', this concerned the love life of Peggy O'Neal, protegée of President Andrew Jackson. It was one of eight films Stewart made in 1936 and happily better things were on the way.

wrong – the reviewer for the London *Observer* told his readers:

What I liked best about the picture was the performance of Mr James Stewart . . . he acts Gable and Harlow off the screen. He is one of those young moderns of whom you feel, with a start of surprise, that good actors don't stop with your generation – they keep right on coming.

After a bit part in *Small Town Girl* with Janet Gaynor and Robert Young, Stewart gained his first starring role in *Speed*, Hollywood's response to Malcolm Campbell's world automobile speed record in September 1935. It was essentially a small budget B-picture but it did Stewart's career no harm and he did learn a very valuable piece of advice from Ted Healy, an old character actor:

He told me to think of the audience not simply as watchers but as collaborators, as sort of partners in the project. He was right and that helped me in my attitude toward the business.

Stewart's next appearance on film was a step upward, a good role in MGM's big Christmas offering for 1936, *After the Thin Man*, with William Powell and Myrna Loy. He played a shy, amiable young man who continues to love a woman who has left him to marry a bounder. The latter becomes a suspect in her murder and William Powell sleuths out the surprising truth – that Stewart is in fact the murderer. Stewart gives a fine Jekyll-to-Hyde performance when he is discovered but his genial, everybody's friend image took a knock in this picture, and

the Stewart *persona* was not yet sufficiently firmly established for such a turnaround. Stewart made eight films in 1936 and acted alongside some very big stars including William Powell, Jean Harlow, Clark Gable, Robert Taylor, Franchot Tone and Eleanor Powell. The film he made with Powell, *Born to Dance*, was a follow-up to her successful *Broadway Melody of 1936*. The movie featured several Cole Porter songs and the composer himself chose Stewart to be Powell's leading man. This lighthearted piece of musical entertainment was just what 1930s audiences wanted to see and the film was a popular success. Stewart even got to sing a Cole Porter song; he croons 'Easy to Love' to Eleanor Powell from a park bench. He has always deprecated his singing efforts but in fact his delivery is light and charming – far worse singers have made a living in Hollywood.

James Stewart and Henry Fonda were now sharing a Mexican-style farmhouse in Brentwood, Hollywood. They were looked after there by an idiosyncratic elderly couple who made a habit of filling up the bath with milk for the local wild cats. Greta Garbo lived next door and her new neighbors were desperate to get a peak at the legendary star. She had an eight-foot fence built to keep out prying eyes – eyes that just occasionally belonged to Fonda and Stewart. Jimmy did not share his friend's dissatisfaction with the studio system. In 1979, looking back on his life as an MGM contract player, he remembered it as hard work:

*Right:* Stewart had a bit part in *Small Town Girl* (1936) with Janet Gaynor (pictured here) and Robert Taylor, one of his fellow players at MGM and another up-and-coming star.

If you weren't making tests with new people the studios were thinking of signing then you were in the gym working out, or taking lessons. Getting out exploiting pictures you weren't in or beating the drum for motion pictures.

MGM knew that they were on to a good thing with Stewart but still weren't quite sure what to do with him, and he had to compete with many other first rate talents signed to the studio, Clark Gable, Franchot Tone, Melvyn Douglas, Robert Montgomery and Spencer Tracy among them. The MGM publicity department released the usual folksy, clichéd information about the young Stewart and the tone was set right from the start: ' . . . the up-right, average product of a small American town and God-fearing parents . . . endowed with a keen sense of humor.' The studio were often very imaginative in their attempts to make their young hopefuls into stars, but in Stewart's case there was no need – the man was his image. One young fan hit the nail on the head when she wrote to him saying 'I like you because you're like the boy next door.' As for his private life, Stewart was happy to resist his

father's ambition for him to marry and settle down. He developed a tendency to fall a little in love with his leading ladies but gradually grew out of this star-struck habit. Alex Stewart may not have found his son a wife but he did find him a church when, on a visit to Jimmy in Hollywood, he realized he was no longer attending church every Sunday. The dutiful son joined the congregation of the Brentwood Presbyterian Church.

Stewart was loaned out to Twentieth Century Fox for his first film of 1937. *Seventh Heaven* was directed by the veteran Henry King and co-starred the French actress Simone Simon. It was not right for Stewart and was disliked by both critics and public, who were not too keen on James Stewart, the American's American, playing a French sew-age worker. Two much more suitable and successful pictures followed, *The Last Gangster* and *Navy Blue and Gold.* Both gave Stewart just the right kind of role – decent, clean-cut, attractive young men with the necessary heroic attributes. In *Navy Blue and Gold* Stewart was able to realize a childhood dream and attend the United States Naval Academy

*Below:* Stewart declares his love for Eleanor Powell in the Cole Porter depression musical *Born to Dance* (1936). Porter himself chose Stewart for the role of Powell's leading man in this audience-pleasing picture, and Stewart was actually given a Cole Porter number, 'Easy to Love' to sing – he carried it off with style.

at Annapolis. In 1937 movies about the armed forces were expected to beat the patriotic drum and this one, which co-starred Robert Walker, did so loud and clear. With a plot involving romance, US football and young naval cadets, *Navy Blue and Gold* could not fail and Howard Barnes, reviewing for the *New York Herald*, was one of many who singled out Stewart for praise:

. . . He breathes life into his character and holds a formularized theme to a strict pattern. It is due to his expert rendition of a rather preposterous part that a rather preposterous show becomes generally exciting.

Stewart next took on a major role in *Of Human Hearts*, a somber drama of frontier life in pre-Civil War days. His part as the rebellious son of Walter Huston's circuit preacher was an important first step into what was to become very much his territory: American myth and the forging of the American spirit. The director George Stevens was responsible for Stewart's first venture into comedy when he cast him in his film *Vivacious Lady* with Ginger Rogers. Stewart played a midwestern college professor

who is sent to New York to rescue a wayward cousin from the clutches of avaricious city slickers. He meets a sophisticated nightclub singer, Rogers, falls in love, and marries her. The film focuses on the comedy of Rogers' efforts to adjust to Stewart's very different way of life. *The New York Times'* critic thought Stewart's role in the film a 'priceless bit of casting.' The film was a commercial hit for RKO and the same critic astutely summed up Stewart's growing success: 'I've liked James Stewart's face since the first time I saw it and it wears well and gets better, probably because he has in himself the true qualities he must describe.' These qualities – a combination of stubbornness, sensitivity and strength of character – were to be portrayed by Stewart again and again.

*The Shopworn Angel* was Stewart's opening film of 1938 and his second with co-star Margaret Sullavan. This is a highly sentimental piece even for 1938 but Stewart and Sullavan work very well together on screen and the movie helped to stamp Stewart on the minds of the film-going public. His role as a naïve, country-boy soldier who falls in love with the gold-

**Below:** Stewart was loaned out to RKO for the Ginger Rogers comedy *Vivacious Lady*, directed by George Stevens in 1938. Stewart plays a stuffy academic who falls in love with a vivacious, blonde show girl (Rogers). Critics were impressed by Stewart's light touch and comic timing.

**Right:** Stewart and Ginger Rogers in another scene from *Vivacious Lady*.

**Below:** Stewart made his second love story with Margaret Sullavan, a friend from his days in the University Players, in 1938. *The Shopworn Angel* was a First World War drama in which they played star-crossed lovers. The critic for the *New York Herald* wrote that Stewart and Sullavan were 'two of the finest actors appearing on the screen today.'

digging Sullavan and marries her, only to die fighting in Europe during the First World War, brings out all Stewart's vulnerable charm.

1938 and 1939 were very important years in James Stewart's career, with the release of three of his most popular and enduring classics, *Destry Rides Again* and *Mr Smith Goes to Washington*, as well as *You Can't Take It With You*. This last was Stewart's first major success and he could not fail to benefit from appearing in such an enjoyable, much-loved picture. It was the first of a trio of wonderful films with director Frank Capra, who found in Stewart exactly the man he needed to realize the male heroism of his vision of the American dream. As Capra expressed it:

I had seen Jimmy Stewart playing a sensitive, heart-stopping role in MGM's *Of Human Hearts*. I sensed the character and rock-ribbed honesty of Gary Cooper, plus the breeding and intelligence of an Ivy League Idealist.

The film was based on the very successful Broadway play by George S Kaufman and Moss Hart which won the Pulitzer Prize. Stewart was quite content to receive third billing behind Jean Arthur and Lionel Barrymore in his role as Tony Kirby, a decent, diffident, wealthy young man who falls for his secretary Alice (Jean Arthur). Alice's grandfather is the loveable, eccentric retired business man (Barrymore) who presides over the wacky Vanderhof family in their rambling, big house where 'everybody knows exactly what to do.' Grandpa Vanderhof has made up his mind long since that money is very much over-valued and the only things that really matter are the ones that you can take with you – love and friendship. The house is full of odd people:

there are Grandpa's friends, including a Russian choreographer and Mr Poppins who invents ingenious toys in the cellar; then there is the immediate family, which consists of the eldest daughter Penny, who writes plays, her husband Paul, who makes fireworks, and their children Essie (Ann Miller), a would-be ballerina, and Alice herself, the only one who struggles to make a living in the outside world.

Edward Arnold plays Stewart's tycoon father who comes to dinner with his wife and is thrown into a state of shock by the Vanderhofs' unusual domestic arrangements. The comedy reaches it peak when everyone ends up in court, after the police turn up to investigate explosions in the cellar. An embarrassed Alice leaves home and Grandpa Vanderhof agrees to sell his house to Kirby senior, who wants it as part of a huge real estate development plan. Tony is offered the presidency of one of his father's firms but turns it down – he has decided to choose gentle eccentricity over ruthless big business. He asks Alice to marry him and displays a little gentle eccentricity himself in the proposal scene, only managing to say at the last moment: 'One little detail I forgot to mention – Alice, I love you.' His father is so impressed that he does not after all buy the Vanderhof home and Alice agrees to marry Tony. Stewart reveals fine comic timing and his usual likeable affability in the role of Tony and, although obviously dated in appearance, the film's humor and charm are timeless.

*You Can't Take It With You* won the Best Picture and Best Director Oscars for 1938. It was Stewart's sixteenth film and one which marked him out as an irreplaceable talent. Stewart's naturalistic, 'non-acting' style is unique to him. The essence of his art lies in his believability, a quality which can be singled out from his other great virtues as an actor such as presence, integrity and comic skills. As the critic of the *New Statesman* wrote in his review of *It's a Wonderful Life*, Stewart defies the notion of acting as lying: 'No actor on the screen today manages to appear more unconscious of script, camera and director than Mr Stewart.' He and Frank Capra were made for each other, as they happily both realized. 'One might believe,' wrote the director, 'that young Stewart could reject his father's patrimony – a kingdom on Wall Street.' With a little help from the great Capra, Jimmy Stewart had made it to the top at thirty years of age.

*Below:* In 1938 Stewart made the first of three classic films with director Frank Capra, whom he credited as the man who made him a star. *You Can't Take It With You* was a delightful and very successful movie. Jean Arthur is seen below with Stewart in a scene from the movie. She played his girlfriend and secretary, a role she reprised in Stewart's second film with Capra, *Mr Smith Goes to Washington*, the following year.

© C.P. CORP. D. COL. 16-389

# Chapter 3
# DESTRY GOES TO WAR
# *1938-1945*

STEWART made his next film out on loan to the maverick producer David O Selznick. In *Made For Each Other* (1939), he starred opposite the gifted Carole Lombard in a contrived melodrama that met with modest critical and commercial success. It was pure art in comparison to his second release of 1939: *Ice Follies of 1939* was pure folly all round. Joan Crawford's career was stumbling and some idiot at MGM thought this ice musical would help revive it. The plan failed miserably, as Crawford was all too well aware: '. . . it was a catastrophe. The public thought so too.' It was with his fourth film of 1939 that Stewart struck gold. His second collaboration with Frank Capra produced another great classic, *Mr Smith Goes to Washington*. Although many people in Hollywood thought Capra would ask for Gary Cooper, the director knew only Stewart could play the naïve, innocent, morally inexhaustible Smith. It is the role with which Stewart is most easily identified; his portrayal of Jefferson Smith made his previous parts look like a preparation for this particular film, so perfect is his rendition of American idealism and belief in the sanctity of democracy and freedom. In an interview with Peter Bogdanovich, Capra described how Stewart became Mr Smith:

It was either Cooper or Stewart and Jim was younger and I knew he would make a hell of a Mr Smith – he looked like the country kid, the idealist – it was very close to him. I think there's no question but that this picture shaped the public image of him, of the real Jimmy Stewart.

Jefferson Smith is the idol of Montana's youth, head of the Boy Rangers and the man behind their *Boys' Stuff* newspaper. When the state senator dies, Smith is chosen by the corrupt party machine to go to Washington and carry on the dead man's work. The party bosses want him to be their obedient lapdog but they don't know who they have taken on in Smith. Clarissa Saunders (Jean Arthur) is sent along as Smith's secretary to keep an eye on him. Claude Rains plays the rotten senator Joseph Paine, a man for whom Smith has a lot of respect as he was a colleague of Smith's dead father.

*Opposite:* A charming 1938 studio portrait of the thirty-year-old Jimmy Stewart.

*Below:* Jimmy takes a closer look at the medium which has made him a star.

**Right:** Stewart and co-star Carole Lombard in *Made for Each Other* (1939), a modestly successful melodrama produced by the maverick movie maker David O Selznick.

**Below:** Somehow, MGM managed to persuade Joan Crawford into starring in *Ice Follies of 1939*, a ludicrous ice dance musical which roped in James Stewart and Lew Ayres as Crawford's ice partners.

Jefferson Smith is inevitably out of place in the big city. He is mocked and derided by those far more foolish than he and is shy and gauche in his attempts to win the senator's daughter. But he is fiercely articulate and forceful when he speaks about the importance of liberty and the free democratic process to Clarissa: 'Liberty is too precious a thing to be buried in books, Miss Saunders' he tells her. 'Men should hold it up in front of them every single day of their lives and say: "I'm free to think and to speak. My ancestors couldn't, I can and my children will".' He grows and matures as the film progresses and wins the love of Jean Arthur's Clarissa Saunders. He realizes that the principles of freedom and justice sometimes have to be defended against those who would deprive others of their right to honest democratic representation. Clarissa feels ashamed of her part in the deception of Smith and confesses all that she knows to him. She reveals that the Claude Rains character has become morally bankrupt and is on the take. Smith is presenting a bill for his pet project, a national boy's camp, without knowing the scheme is a front for Paine and his cohorts, who want to get their hands on the land set aside for the camp in order to line their own pockets. Fearful that their trickery is about to be exposed, the party organizes a cleverly devised smear campaign against Smith, who is shattered when people fall for the lie that he only wants to present the bill for his own financial gain. Clarissa has to persuade Smith that he must fight back. The climax of the film is Smith's effort to right this wrong. He embarks on a marathon talk session, twenty three hours long, on the floor of the Senate to win time for the results of his own investigation in to the corruption to reach him. His speech ends with the words:

You think I'm licked. You all think I'm licked. Well, I'm not licked and I'm going to stay here and fight for this lost cause even if this room gets full of

**Left:** A bemused Mr Smith receives a hero's welcome from some of Washington's young ladies when he arrives at the capital. *Mr Smith Goes to Washington* was Stewart's most important film to date and the role with which he is most closely identified even to this day. It brought him a first, well-deserved Academy Award nomination.

**Below:** An exhausted Smith is congratulated by his fellow senators in the triumphant climax to *Mr Smith Goes to Washington.*

lies like these, and the Taylors and all their armies come marching into this place. Someone will listen to me. Some . . . '

His doggedness wins the admiration of Joseph Paine who steps forward when Smith collapses, admitting: 'All that boy says is true.' Purity of faith has triumphed over ruthless cynicism. Jefferson Smith's trip to Washington handed Stewart a rare opportunity to show just what he could do and no one could have matched it. It is impossible to imagine any other actor carrying off the difficult, delicate scene where Smith decides to leave town and visits Lincoln's tomb, sits down on it and sobs with his head in his hands.

The huge set of the Senate chamber was an exact reconstruction which, in the scene of Smith's triumph, placed Stewart standing amid 96 desks. The hoarseness in the actor's voice was faked by swabbing it each day with a vile mercury mixture that swelled and irritated his vocal chords. The critics were unanimous in liking the film and praising Stewart's performance. The critic for *The Nation* spoke for many when he wrote that Stewart was now eminent among Hollywood actors:

Now he is mature and gives a difficult part, with many nuances, moments of tragic-comic impact. And he is able to do more than play isolated scenes effectively. He shows the strength of a character through experience. In the end he is so forceful that his victory is thoroughly credible. One can only hope that after this success Mr Stewart will remain as uncorruptible as Mr Smith.

The film was a great success across the world
but it was the year of *Gone With The Wind* or
*Mr Smith* would have earned his creators more
than their one Oscar statuette, awarded to
Lewis R Stone for his original screen play. Between them, Stewart and Gable were expected
to walk away with the Oscar for Best Actor,
but Robert Donat won it for his role as the
school master in *Goodbye Mr Chips*.

*Mr Smith Goes to Washington* was a hard act
to follow but *Destry Rides Again* is a delightful,
memorable film in its own right. Released only
two months after the Capra classic, it was the
ideal opportunity to consolidate Stewart's
leading man status and his reputation as the
all-American, small-town hero. The film also
relaunched the career of its other star, Marlene
Dietrich, who had been away from the screen
for two years following a string of disappointing romantic dramas. She took an immediate
liking to Stewart and a brief affair developed
between the two. Marlene received top billing
(how many actors would have been courteous
enough to allow that after such a success as *Mr
Smith?*), and they made an unusual, exciting
pairing: the exotic, foreign, woman of the
world seduced by the quintessentially
American goodness of the Stewart character.

*Destry Rides Again* is a remarkable achievement and a milestone in the careers of those who made it. Directed by George Marshall, it succeeds on several levels. It is a well-timed spoof of the western genre which, by 1939, was a little stale, and is also a clever comedy, drama and musical, as well as retaining the best features of the western. The film contains one of the most famous of movie songs, 'Go See What the Boys in the Backroom Will Have,' and a celebrated film brawl between Dietrich and the wife of one of the men she attracts. The role of Tom Destry continued the Stewart theme of the honest, true man placed in the midst of the avarice and amorality of others whom he must defeat.

The wide-open town of Bottleneck needs a new sheriff, when the old one dies before his term of office expires. Kent (Brian Donlevy), is the crooked boss of the town who picks the local drunk Wash Dimsdale (Charles Winninger) as the replacement. But Wash preempts Kent's plans by choosing Tom Destry, the man with the enviable reputation of having cleaned up the notorious town of Tombstone, to be his deputy. Tom Destry is a very different man from Jefferson Smith in the vital respect that Destry only pretends to be naïve. In fact he is a shrewd man who understands both the good and bad side of human nature. But he is content to let others, less perceptive than he, see only his pleasant, amiable exterior.

When Destry is travelling on the stage coach into Bottleneck a fellow passenger, disbelieving what he sees, asks him if he really is the renowned Destry. 'Folks is always asking me that,' replies Stewart with a smile. Marlene Dietrich is Frenchy, a singer in the Last Chance Saloon, a bar owned, along with everything else, by Kent. She and Destry are drawn to each other by their shared sense of humor. Destry does not carry a gun and explains his reasons to a man who challenges him about it: 'You see, if I had a gun, one of us might have got hurt, and it could have been me.' Frenchy is quick-witted enough to hand him a broom saying that is the only cleaning up Destry is going to be doing around Bottleneck. She falls in love with him when she sees the honesty and courage beneath the simple man act and Destry comes to appreciate the good beneath her painted exterior. Events come to the boil when Wash Dimsdale, who has cleaned up to become a good sheriff, is shot in the back and killed. Destry had hoped to drive

*Below:* Marlene Dietrich and a quizzical-looking James Stewart in a scene from the marvelous *Destry Rides Again* (1939), Stewart's first western and the perfect follow-up to *Mr Smith Goes to Washington*. Stewart and Dietrich had eyes for each other off screen as well as on.

*Right:* Eye to eye with Marlene Dietrich as Frenchy in the aptly named Last Chance Saloon from *Destry Rides Again*. Stewart was gracious enough to allow Dietrich top billing in the picture, even though it followed his great success as Jefferson Smith and was seen as something of a comeback picture for his exotic co-star.

out the villains without resorting to violence, but now his eyes blaze with fury as he straps on his guns and leads the good men of the town into the saloon for a showdown with Kent and his men. Frenchy joins in the action by marching the townswomen down the main street to protect their men. Tom finds Kent and kills him but he is not the only one to die. Frenchy deliberately gets in the way of a bullet meant for Stewart and dies in his arms.

1939 was a good year for the western; audiences were treated to *Stagecoach*, *Jesse*

*Right:* Margaret Sullavan, James Stewart and Frank Morgan in the delicate Ernst Lubitsch comedy *The Little Shop Around the Corner* (1939), set somewhat improbably in Budapest.

*James* (which starred Henry Fonda), and *Union Pacific*. Critics loved *Destry* which was a personal triumph for Stewart. The scene where this unlikely hero is first seen by the sceptical people of Bottleneck, as he climbs out of the stagecoach holding a parasol and a birdcage for a lady passenger, is just one where his indefinable talent shines. Movie critic Bosley Crowther had no doubts about Stewart's work in the film:

It was a masterpiece of underplaying in a deliberately sardonic vein – the freshest, most offbeat characterization that this popular actor has ever played. It was, in my mind, even better than the rampant young senator in *Mr Smith*.

James Stewart is one of Hollywood's best loved figures. *Destry* was just one film in which he endeared himself to the crew with his unfailing politeness and lack of temperament. Marlene Dietrich found him equally easy to work with: 'I never had so much fun working in Hollywood as when I was working with Jimmy. He's a sweet human being.' Mike Chaffney was a studio electrician in the *Destry* crew. He was returning to work after the recent death of his wife from cancer, and greatly appreciated Stewart taking time to listen to him and have a few sympathetic words.

Stewart returned to MGM and conventional drama with Ernst Lubitsch's bittersweet romance *The Little Shop Around the Corner*. This was Stewart's third and best film with Margaret Sullavan. He plays the head sales-

man in a leather shop in Budapest and Sullavan is the young sales girl he takes on as a beginner. Completely unwittingly, the two have become pen pals, a fact Stewart discovers halfway through the picture. The film was not the box office attraction it might have been had the story been transplanted to an American town. Stewart was never quite right in foreign roles; his identity was too uniquely American. His next film was a case in point – *The Mortal Storm* was his last movie with Margaret Sullavan and his first film to be released

*Right:* The scene everyone remembers from *The Philadelphia Story* (1940) and perhaps Stewart's most romantic on-screen moment. Mike Connor carries a tipsy Tracy Lord (Katharine Hepburn) back from a moonlight swim on the night before her planned wedding to another man. She has fallen gladly off the pedestal that her stuffy fiancé had placed her on and into Connor's arms – but will she marry him?

in 1940. It was part of a growing Hollywood trend to condemn what was happening in Nazi Germany and seems out of place in today's world, but it is still interesting to observe the special relationship Stewart and Sullavan had on the big screen.

*No Time For Comedy* is another film that belongs in the 'they don't make them like that any more' category. Stewart and his co-star Rosalind Russell were adept at the kind of acting required for this romantic piece of fluff, which tells the tale of a stuffy playwright (Stewart) who writes a surprise comedy hit, then tries to return to serious plays without success. He falls in love with the leading lady of his first hit play and takes her advice to stick

**Left:** Ruth Hussey, James Stewart and an especially interested Cary Grant look on as Katharine Hepburn receives the letter from her fiancé that tells her the wedding is off. Not easily deterred, Hepburn simply marries someone else – her ex-husband, Cary Grant, the man who still loves her.

**Below:** *The Philadelphia Story* brought Stewart his first and only Oscar. Here he is seen with Ginger Rogers, winner in the Best Actress stakes for her title role in *Kitty Foyle*, at the 1941 Academy Awards dinner.

with comedy plays in the future. The film pleased audiences and Stewart, as usual, pleased the critics. Bosley Crowther wrote in his *New York Times* review:

Mr Stewart is the best thing in the picture – a completely ingratiating character who ranges from the charming clumsiness of a country playwright to the temperamental distraction of an established writer with complete natural assurance.

Surprisingly it was James Stewart and not Katherine Hepburn who won an Oscar for *The Philadelphia Story*, although it was very much a Hepburn picture. It was hoped (with good reason as it turned out) that the film would be a successful box office come back for her career, which had slipped somewhat after a flying start in the early 1930s. She had made the play a great success for the Theater Guild and MGM took on both Hepburn and the script as a package deal. Part of the agreement was that Hepburn could call the shots and she wanted the best. She wisely chose George Cukor, who had directed her in four of her most popular successes, *A Bill of Divorcement*, *Little Women*, *Sylvia Scarlett* and *Holiday*. Although she originally wanted Spencer Tracy and Clark Gable as her leading men Hepburn was quite willing to settle for Cary Grant and James Stewart.

The Philadelphia Story is basically the love life of Tracy Lord, a fine example of what the Stewart character calls 'the rich, rapacious, American female.' Stewart plays Mike Con-

*Above:* Not every Stewart picture could be a classic and *Ziegfeld Girl* (1941), which co-starred Judy Garland and a young Lana Turner, certainly wasn't. Choreographed by Busby Berkeley, it was a no more than adequate big-budget drama about the professional and emotional problems of Ziegfeld chorus girls.

nor, a hard-up short story writer who works as a journalist for *Spy* magazine. He and a photographer Liz Imbrie (Ruth Hussey), who is secretly in love with him, arrive at the Lord mansion to cover the society wedding of Tracy and her stuffy, unsuitable coal millionaire fiancé George Kitteridge (John Howard). Connor and Imbrie have little time for this feasting of the idle rich. Cary Grant is Tracy's playboyish ex-husband C K Dexter. He is still in love with her and knows she is about to make a mistake, so he has organized the presence of *Spy* magazine at the wedding in the hope that it will cause problems. He has informed the owners of the magazine of the marital indiscretions of Tracy's father, who has been unwillingly persuaded to allow *Spy* the prized exclusive rights to report Tracy's wedding. Dexter's clever plan goes a little awry when Connor falls in love with Tracy and she, momentarily, with him. Connor despises the social set and its wanton, elegant lifestyle but he learns the wisdom of the Spanish proverb he quotes, 'With the rich and mighty, a little patience.' This is quite a change in attitude from his earlier remark that 'the prettiest sight in this pretty world is the privileged class enjoying its privileges.' It is Connor's discovery of the real Tracy Lord that brings about this

change. He realizes Tracy is more than just a rich, spoilt young woman once he sees the intelligent, vital, very special girl underneath. Mike Connor speaks the most romantic words ever uttered by Stewart on screen when he eulogizes Tracy:

There's a magnificence in you, Tracy, . . . the magnificence that comes out of your eyes and your voice and the way you stand there and the way you walk. You're lit from within, Tracy. You've got fires banked down in you, hearth fires and holocausts.

This glowing tribute spills out of Connor when he and Tracy drink a little too much at the pre-wedding party and take a moonlight, nude swim in the pool. This and other problems cause Kitteridge to call off the wedding just when the ceremony is about to begin. Connor offers to take his place but Tracy gently turns him down in favor of her true love Dexter (and she knows that an anxious Liz is standing on the side lines). So Stewart ends up the loser in love and has to watch his 'golden girl, full of love and warmth and delight' marry another man. But on Oscar night Stewart was the winner. George Cukor, Katherine Hepburn and Ruth Hussey were all nominated in their respective categories but only Stewart walked away with one of the famous statuettes. He had cast his vote for Henry Fonda, who was nominated for his role as Judd Hoad in *The Grapes of Wrath*. Fonda's performance was indeed a great one and some people, including Stewart himself, felt that the Best Actor Oscar awarded to Stewart was a compensation for losing out for *Mr Smith Goes to Washington*. Stewart has stated that he does not consider he was a very worthy winner but then he is a very modest man. He was full of praise for his co-stars Hepburn and Grant:

When you work with Grant and Hepburn, you work! You let up for a second and they'll steal the movie from under your nose. Talent like that keeps you on your toes.

*The Philadelphia Story* was a huge box office hit but lost out to Hitchcock's *Rebecca* for Best Picture Oscar. Alex Stewart certainly had no doubts about his son's award. For years he had felt trepidation over Jimmy's acting career, always taking care to remind him that J M Stewart and Sons would be there if ever Hollywood let him down and he needed a real job. In the end it was Hollywood that came to the hardware store when Alex proudly placed his son's Oscar in the shop window in Indiana. Stewart had starred in three more movies by the time he picked up his Academy Award on February 1941 at the Biltmore Hotel in Los Angeles. They were all relatively minor efforts – *Come Live With Me*, *Pot O' Gold*, *Ziegfeld Girl*. *Come Live With Me* was the most enjoyable. Directed by Clarence Brown and co-starring the lovely Hedy Lamarr, the picture

*Left:* James Stewart was one of the very first of the Hollywood movie stars to enlist for the Second World War. Here he is seen, with a new short hair cut, taking the Army Oath in May 1941.

was another romantic comedy which did well enough to please MGM and fans of the two stars, who could sit back and enjoy Stewart's appealing performance and Hedy's beautiful face.

Stewart's mind was now concentrated on something more important to him than acting.

From the time the Second World War had broken out in September 1939, Stewart had spent as many hours as possible flying his two-seater Stinson 105 in order to gain the necessary flying hours to qualify as a military pilot. He strongly resisted MGM's efforts to persuade him to stay at home to fight the war as a movie

84527A.C

*Left:* Stewart served a large part of his Second World War service in Norfolk, England. This is Lieutenant-Colonel James Stewart, Group Operations Officer, interrogating the crew of the 453rd bomb crew after their return from a mission over enemy territory. He also flew many missions himself and was awarded a DFC for his leadership of his squadron in the raid on Brunswick in February 1944.

star. He made his first attempt to enlist in the United States Air Force less than a month after winning his Oscar. He was found lacking in only one thing – weight; it was the old problem of not enough pounds (14 of them) for his very tall height. A slimming specialist reversed his usual practices to encourage Stewart to eat plenty of steaks and fattening steam puddings, which rapidly brought him up to the required standard. He was so determined to pass the medical that he did not allow himself to urinate or have a bowel movement before the examination. He joined up on March 9, 1941, nine months before the Japanese air attack on Pearl Harbor.

His friends Burgess Meredith and Billy Grundy witnessed the moment when Stewart emerged victorious from the induction center. Grundy recalled Stewart's jubilation: 'Suddenly a door flew open and a tall, skinny man in his shorts, carrying his clothes over his arm, ran past us, screaming like a banshee "I'M IN, I'M IN, I'M IN!" He waved goodbye and was off to Fort MacArthur.' After basic training Stewart was posted to Moffet Field Air Corps training base in northern California where, owing to his previous flying experience, he quickly gained his corporal's stripe. He was sent to Kirkland Field where he flew four-engine bombers and made it to the rank of Lieutenant after nine months military service. He wore his new uniform for his appearance at the Academy Award ceremony in February 1942, when he presented Gary Cooper with

*Above:* A proud Major James Stewart receives the Distinguished Flying Cross on May 3, 1944 from Lieutenant-Colonel Ramsey D Potts. Stewart was honored with the award for his leadership of a combat wing of Liberators (B24s) on a bombing mission to Brunswick.

*Right:* A bemedaled Jimmy is greeted by his parents Elizabeth and Alex Stewart, who journeyed to New York to meet their son after his return from the war aboard the liner *Queen Elizabeth*.

the Best Actor Oscar for his role in *Sergeant York*.

Stewart then served as an instructor for 'Flying Fortress' pilots until November 1943 when, as a newly appointed Captain, he arrived in the village of Tibbenham in Norfolk, England, where he served as part of the Second Air Division of the Eighth Air Command. He did his best to avoid the inevitable attentions of the press and to act like just another pilot throughout his time in England, which lasted until the end of the war. Stewart took part in dozens of flying missions, including twenty as captain of his B-24 Liberator. He was Major Stewart by the time he was awarded the Distinguished Flying Cross for his leadership of the 703rd Squadron of bombers during the February 20, 1944 raid on Brunswick; he already held the Air Medal, with Oak Leaf Cluster. On his discharge from service in September 1945, Stewart was promoted to Colonel and Chief of Staff on the Eighth Air Force, Second Combat Wing. He had served his country with honor and clocked up 18,000 flying hours.

Jimmy wanted to make a quiet return to Indiana but of course he was greeted with a hero's welcome. The town mayor had even organized a reporter from *Life* magazine (shades of Mike Connor in *The Philadelphia Story*) to be there to report the homecoming. When Stewart had said goodbye to his father before departing for England in 1943, Alex Stewart had given his son an envelope containing a farewell note and a copy of the Ninety First Psalm. The gift proved to be more than just a poignant gesture for, as Stewart recalled, he had reason to turn to his father's wisdom on one particular night:

Our group had suffered heavy casualties during the day, and the next morning at dawn I would have to lead my squadron out again, deep into enemy territory. Imagination can become a soldier's worst enemy. Fear is an insidious, deadly thing; it can warp judgement, freeze reflexes and breed mistakes. Worse, it's contagious. I knew my own fear, if not checked, could infect my crew members, and I could feel it growing in me. I remembered talking to my father when I was a boy and asking him about his experiences in World War One and the Spanish American War. I had asked him if he had been afraid. He said: "Everybody is son, but just remember you can't handle fear all by yourself. Give it to God. He'll carry it for you". I reread the Ninety First Psalm that my father had given me and when I left, I felt comforted, felt I had done all I could.

Stewart has been taciturn about his war-time experiences and insisted that a clause be inserted in any post-war contract to the effect that his part in the Second World War would never be used to promote a film in any way. He has always refused to appear in any jingoistic, exploitative war films.

Four years is a long time to be away from Hollywood. The case brought by Olivia de Havilland against Warner Brothers had changed the relationship between the studios and their stars. Actors could no longer be forced to complete contracts that would have lapsed had it not been for unforeseen circumstances such as enforced absence or illness. Friends of Stewart's such as Gary Cooper and Henry Fonda were now working as freelances. Stewart's old doubts about the value of acting had returned – no intelligent man could return from a war unchanged. He surprised Louis B Mayer by rejecting his proposal to take up the one and a half years left to run on his contract (years that had gone by during the war). Robert Taylor and Clark Gable were happy to be welcomed back into MGM's safe arms but Stewart no longer wanted to be a contract player, and was never one again. Months went by and nothing much happened until Stewart received a phone call from his old partner Frank Capra, who wondered whether Stewart might be interested in a tall tale of a family man with problems, who is saved by a second-class angel called Clarence . . .

*Above:* Stewart with Clark Gable – two Army Air Corps Lieutenants who just happen to be major movie stars meet in Hollywood for the first time since they both joined the war effort.

# Chapter 4
# A WONDERFUL LIFE
# 1946-1955

I t's a Wonderful Life (RKO 1946) is a classic piece of American film history. Like Stewart, Frank Capra was home from the war and anxious to make his own way artistically. He formed Liberty Films with director William Wyler and producer Samuel Briskin. *It's a Wonderful Life* was their first project. It began life as a Philip Van Doren Stern short story about a man who finds his life transformed by a timely intervention from above. George Bailey (James Stewart) is fed up with his lot after twenty years of humdrum, small-town existence in Bedford Falls. He once had grand ambitions to see and conquer the world but his father's sudden death just when he was set to go off to college thwarted his plans. George is a good, kind man who did the decent thing and stayed at home to take over the running of the family's building and loan company. He has to watch his chances slip by and see his younger brother rise to fame as a football star. He marries the lovely Mary Hatch (Donna Reed), one of his few pieces of good fortune, but they have to forego a honeymoon when the money is needed to save the business in an unexpected crisis. His poor hearing confines him to serving as an air raid warden during the Second World War while his brother Harry is decorated by the President for gallantry in combat.

The last straw in George's lot comes on the day his absent-minded uncle misplaces a vital sum of money, which falls into the hands of H C Potter (Lionel Barrymore). Potter is George's nemesis and has long had his greedy eyes on the Baileys' company; he already owns everything else of any great worth in Bedford Falls. George is facing scandal and financial ruin at the hands of Potter. He decides suicide is the answer and jumps off a bridge into the local river, but fails to drown himself because he is forced to save an elderly man from drowning. Clarence Oddbody later explains to a con-

*Left:* The scene from *It's a Wonderful Life* where George (Stewart) has to step in to keep the grasping hands of H C Potter off his father's building and loan company. George's Uncle Billy (Thomas Mitchell) whose bumbling will later land George in even deeper trouble, is among those looking on as George emphasizes his point to the scheming Potter (played by Lionel Barrymore).

*Below:* Stewart in Capra's *Magic Town* (1947). A whimsical comedy about an opinion pollster who discovers a small town which exactly mirrors the views of the USA, it lacked the great director's normally magical touch.

fused George that he threw himself into the river at the same time in order to rescue George from his disillusionment with life. He is a second-class guardian angel intent on finally gaining his wings, which he hopes to do by saving poor George. Clarence shows George how Bedford Falls would look if he had never been born, and it is a pretty dismal picture. His brother Harry would have died in childhood (George rescued him from drowning when Harry fell into an icy lake) and Potter would control everything – the town would even be renamed Pottersville. The many townspeople who only have their own homes thanks to the Bailey company would still be at the mercy of Potter as they were before George intervened. George returns home where, unknown to him, his many friends have rallied round to collect enough money to save him and his company from Potter, who appears to be the only bad man in Bedford Falls.

*It's a Wonderful Life* is a perfectly achieved, richly detailed American fairy tale. George Bailey was not an easy role to play. He is quite an extreme character and it took Stewart's mastery of the art of film acting to convey the stubborness, tenderness, kind heart and lost hope that make up George. At the beginning of the film, he is a young man full of enthusiasm and joy for life but he becomes (until the very end, of course) a disappointed, jealous man who shouts abuse at his wife and children and blames Mary for having too many kids. In

*Above:* James Stewart and Lee J Cobb in a scene from *Call Northside 777*, a tough, high-quality suspense drama from 1948 which saw Stewart take on a new, harder-edged role which was to be the first of many.

*Opposite:* Stewart receives a few pointers from Alfred Hitchcock on the set of *Rope* (1948), their first film together.

the scene where George confronts his uncle about the mislaid money, Stewart gets the chance to show how well he could portray anger and cold resentment, emotions not then associated with the Stewart *persona*. His temper erupts as he grabs the old man's lapel and warns: 'One of us is going to jail and it isn't going to be me.' Capra had found Stewart 'older, shyer, ill at ease' after his absence from the film world but the talent was still very much there. *It's a Wonderful Life* was a triumphant return to movie acting for Stewart; he was nominated for his third Academy Award but Fredric March won it for his performance in *The Best Years of Our Lives*, which also beat Capra's film in the Best Film stakes. For such a much-loved, enduring favorite, however, *It's a Wonderful Life* was a surprising box office disappointment at the time, failing to recoup the $2 million it cost to make – a vast sum for movie-making in 1946. Despite this the film is the personal favorite of both Stewart and Capra. In 1977, Stewart acknowledged his debt to Capra:

In my opinion, Capra is one of the giants of the picture business and always will be. It is amazing the contribution that he made to the industry when it was young and just getting on its feet – Frank had a great deal to do with the progress of my career over the years and I will always be grateful to him.

Stewart's post-war good fortune did not continue with *Magic Town*, a Capraesque piece of whimsy that was an artistic flop. The script had been written especially for Stewart by Robert Riskin, who was responsible for several of Capra's best pictures including *You Can't Take It With You*, and *Mr Deeds Goes To Town*. Stewart acknowledged a lesson learnt: 'I've not time for movies written especially for me. This was one and it wasn't so hot.' Some reviewers shared Stewart's worry that he was in danger of playing it too safe with yet another film about life in small-town America. One critic even went so far as to wonder how long he would have to put up with this 'long beanstalk, humming and hawing all over the place' – probably the unkindest words ever written about James Stewart's film acting.

Stewart knew he had to review his career. It was time to take a risk, and *Call Northside 777* was just what he needed. This gritty, documentary-style drama was based on fact; Stewart played the first of his real-life characters, a Chicago journalist called James McGuire (his name was changed to Mickey McNeal in the picture). Director Henry Hathaway took his whole team to Chicago for location shooting, adding to the authenticity of the film. Stewart did not feel any need to immerse himself in the world of journalism: 'I'm not what you call a method actor – I've always been sceptical of people who say they lose themselves in a part.'

The plot begins when McGuire investigates a small ad placed by a Polish cleaning woman, who has scraped together $5000 as a reward for evidence leading to the release of her son (Richard Conte) who is in prison, having been convicted several years earlier of the murder of a policeman. McGuire loses his initial scepticism and comes to believe in the son's innocence. The denouement is tense: Conte's release depends upon a new technique, used to blow up an old photograph and show the date on a newspaper held under someone's arm. The ploy succeeds in discrediting a key witness who testified against Conte at his trial, and Conte is a free man. The film was a welcome hit for Stewart and, even more importantly, it enabled him to toughen up his image; *Call Northside 777* is quite a departure from Stewart's more regular roles as everyone's favorite boy next door.

Hitchcock directed Stewart's next major film, the experimental psychodrama *Rope*. This was a first for Stewart on several counts: his first film in technicolor, and the beginning of his partnership with Alfred Hitchcock. *Rope* is an interesting oddity. The film runs for eighty minutes, also the running time of Patrick Hamilton's successful Broadway play on which the film was based. Hitchcock filmed the scenes in ten minute takes with 'invisible' cuts to create the impression of one continuous

drama. It was a curious decision and in an interview Hitchcock admitted:

I undertook *Rope* as stunt. That's the only way I can describe it, I don't know how I came to indulge in it.

The actors had to learn their lines perfectly (a task Stewart has always found difficult); one fluffed line could ruin these unusual takes. In an interview with George Perry for *The Sunday Times* in 1983, Stewart talked about his initial problems in working with Hitchcock:

He didn't explain what he wanted of the role in *Rope* . . . he expected us to have worked out the characters and how they should be played and he went along with it. If he didn't like it he would come up afterwards and suggest another way for comparison. But he didn't say my way's right and yours is wrong.

On the whole, Stewart felt that the acting suffered as a result of the innovations used to film *Rope*: 'The audiences wanted to be just audiences, they didn't really want to become the eyes of a mobile camera.'

Nevertheless, the film is a clever murder game which pits a teacher against two of his former pupils, who choose the murder of a friend as their battleground. Rupert Cadell (Stewart) is a lecturer in intellectual theory who includes the Nietzschean idea of super-humankind in his teachings. John Dall and Farley Granger play Brandon and Philip, homosexuals who claim to have been in-fluenced by Cadell in their strong contempt for ordinary people (he is their former housemas-ter). They strangle a fellow student and then act out a macabre joke by inviting his and their friends to a party at their penthouse apartment where they place the party food on a chest con-taining the dead man's corpse.

Their deceased friend's non-appearance becomes the focal point of conversation at the gathering and Cadell, who has been invited as a challenge, guesses what has happened. Brandon taunts him to guess how the murder was committed and he does so, even producing the rope used in the crime. This produces a confession from Philip, a more normal charac-ter than the psychotic Brandon. In a splendid close-up, Cadell opens the chest lid and we see his anguish and horror as he says: 'You've given my words a meaning that I never dreamt of – you've tried to twist them into a cold, logical excuse for your ugly murder.' His promise to ensure that they pay for their evil crime de-livers the message of the film, which did not perform too well at the box office.

*Opposite:* Stewart embraces June Allyson, his screen wife in the hugely popular film *The Stratton Story* (1949), which depicted the real-life comeback of heroic baseball pitcher Monty Stratton, who returned to the game after an accident left him with only one leg.

*Below:* Farley Granger, James Stewart and John Dall in the confrontation scene at the end of *Rope*.

**Right:** James Stewart escorts Loretta Young to the preview of *Mr Smith Goes to Washington* in the spring of 1939. Stewart was one of Hollywood's most popular and eligible bachelors before his marriage in 1949 at the age of 41.

**Far right:** Olivia de Havilland and James Stewart, romantic partners for a time in the 1930s, arrive in New York in 1940.

Stewart's post-war career has been dominated by his work with three directors – Alfred Hitchcock, Anthony Mann and John Ford. He made three more films with the master of suspense: the excellent *Rear Window*; the less successful *The Man Who Knew Too Much*; and that masterful study in romantic obsession, *Vertigo*. Director and star held each other in the highest esteem. Hitchcock considered the man some thought of as his alter-ego 'unmatchable yet Mr Everyman', and Stewart has no time for those who criticize the director's oddball personality. He believes he was privileged to work with such a cinematic genius and had these words for those who showed Hitchcock less respect:

He had a quality all his own that I don't think will ever be found in a director again. Recently, there was a derogatory biography about him. It made me feel pity for the author. Hitch's personality, his morality, had nothing to do with his extraordinary skill.

Hitchcock is alleged to have once remarked: 'All actors should be treated like cattle,' and Stewart has joked in response: 'As one of Hitch's cattle, I still think he was great!'

1949 was a very productive year for James Stewart. He returned to the western genre which he had not touched since *Destry*, and it became a medium in which he broke new ground as an actor. The year got off to a good start with the release of a very popular moneys-pinner for Stewart, *The Stratton Story*. Sam Wood directed Stewart in this drama of real-life baseball player Monty Stratton's triumphant return to the game after a hunting accident left him with only one leg. *Variety* ranked the film sixth in their list of the top ten grossing films of 1949. Stratton himself was very pleased with the film and thought Stewart's pitching was excellent – he was coached by the very man he was playing. Critical acclaim was Stewart's once again and he showed he could still project his pre-war image of the country boy who has to fight hard to prove himself in the big city (Stratton was originally a Texan farm boy). June Allyson played Stewart's wife (a case of 5ft 1 inch versus 6ft 3 inches), the first of three films in which they played a married couple. Stewart spent five days receiving instruction from major league baseball players and wore a steel harness for the scenes which required a limp. His success helped Stewart to recover from his last few disappointing films. The *New Republic* said that Stewart played 'the pitching phenomenon from the back country with a pleasant Will Rodgers wit, and in the ball park sequences looks astonishingly professional.'

For many years Stewart had been one of Hollywood's most eligible single men. He later recalled his bachelor days as 'wonderful, just wonderful,' and this is no surprise when one considers that he dated and romanced some of the most beautiful women in Hollywood. Olivia de Havilland, Jean Harlow, Rita Hayworth, Alice Faye, Lana Turner, Marlene

Dietrich, Norma Shearer and Dorothy Lamour were just some of them. 'Who will be Mrs Jimmy Stewart?' was a favorite question in Hollywood's showbusiness press. Between 1935 and 1949 more than a hundred stories concerning Stewart's love life appeared in movie fan magazines. Jimmy's stock answer to questions regarding his single status was polite and to the point: 'Most of the actresses I date are fine women but I'm still looking.' Leland Haywood, Stewart's agent and close friend, tried as hard to find Stewart a wife as he did good acting roles. Alex Stewart was equally keen for his son to marry and settle down, and would quote the Bible at Jimmy: 'It's not good for man to live alone.'

Stewart knew how to enjoy himself while he was 'still looking'; some of the parties he gave with fellow bachelors passed into Hollywood legend. Olivia de Havilland has fond memories of her romance with Stewart. One date was briefly interrupted thanks to Stewart's absent-mindedness. Stewart picked up de Havilland for the evening and then suddenly sprinted after his car, which was beginning to roll down a hill – he had left the handbrake off. Their relationship really had the gossip columns buzzing – Walter Winchell, a famous Hollywood commentator, joked: 'Their first date got more coverage than did Orson Welles' famous *War of the Worlds*'; Stewart escorted de Havilland to the New York premiere of *Gone With the Wind* in which she co-starred. She found him 'such good company to be with – a grown up Huck Finn.' They broke up when everyone was expecting them to marry; Olivia de Havilland believes 'Jimmy wasn't really ready for a wife.'

August 9, 1949 was a black day for the fan magazines, for it was on that date that James Stewart finally took a bride – their GAB (Great American Bachelor) was no more. Stewart was 41 when he married Gloria Hatrick McLean, ex-wife of millionaire Edward McLean. Gloria was ten years younger than Jimmy and not a showbiz professional, but she was no stranger to the entertainment world; she was an ex-model and her father was head of MGM's legal department. Gloria had two sons, Ronald and Michael, aged five and seven, from the first marriage. She was a very attractive, tall woman with large green eyes and wavy brown hair. In her autobiography, June Allyson wrote that she felt the Stewarts were ideally suited to one another: ' . . . both tall and dignified, and both with the same sense of humor.'

There had been only one real obstacle to the Stewarts' romance: Gloria's German Shepherd dog Bellow who lived up to his name when he first met Stewart, taking an immediate dislike to him. It was only after a lot of efforts and dog biscuits from his mistress' suitor that Bellow came round and accepted the situation. The couple honeymooned in Hawaii before moving into their eight-bedroom Tudor-styled house in Beverly Hills, where they have lived ever since (they later bought the house next door as well). Stewart's own words best describe his decision to marry when he did:

**Left:** Stewart and bride-to-be Gloria McLean together during a break from filming *Broken Arrow* in 1949. Their engagement was announced during the making of the film, Stewart's first western since *Destry Rides Again* ten years earlier.

*Right:* Gloria and Jimmy pose for the cameras shortly before their wedding in August 1949.

*Opposite:* Stewart in the role of Lin McAdam, a man hellbent on obsessive revenge in the western *Winchester 73* (1950), his first film with director Anthony Mann. Each proved to be the other's ideal collaborator. The five Stewart/Mann westerns of the 1950s completely turned Jimmy's career around.

'. . . when you're 41, life means more than just a bookful of telephone numbers. I needed the security of a relationship with a woman I loved. I needed a family and I needed to put down roots. I can say all the usual things about meeting the right girl and falling in love but it was also the right time.'

Gloria was not the only person with whom Stewart developed a vital partnership as the new decade, the 1950s, dawned. In teaming up with director Anthony Mann, he was able completely to redirect his career – the 1950s became his most successful decade both commercially and artistically. By 1950 Stewart had been a Hollywood star for 15 years; very few of the young male stars who started out with him were able to endure as he had, and Stewart now managed to find a rich new seam to his talent.

In 1950 Stewart made four good and successful films of which *Winchester 73* and *Broken Arrow*, were by far the most important. Until

then he had nearly always played good-natured, straightforward men in essentially lighthearted pictures. The change in direction was to be a radical one. He did, of course, continue to represent affable, American geniality in many more pictures, but in his movies with Anthony Mann Stewart portrayed wholly new characterizations of deeply flawed, obsessive, morally ambiguous, angry men. Previously only *Mr Smith* had allowed Stewart to exhibit any real rage. In *Winchester 73* the audience saw their homeboy favorite play an embittered, angry man hellbent on revenge. Stewart seized the role gladly – the film was part of a package deal with Universal, who had bought Stewart's hit play *Harvey*, and Stewart signed to make that and the western. He knew he had to change in order to keep up with cinema-going audiences. Westerns were still very popular and the genre was often in need of a strong, moral, leading man. Even so, Stewart could not have foreseen success and the transition was a brave decision which Stewart remembers as a 'desperate move – a life saver.'

Stewart worked very hard to learn to fire a rifle for his role in *Winchester 73* and was thankful that he already knew how to ride: 'I'd always known how to ride – my father'd always had a horse and insisted I learn how to ride and this kind of stood me in good stead.' *Winchester 73* was actually made before *Broken Arrow* and released later as its subject matter was considered much more controversial. *Broken Arrow* was the first of a small group of important, revisionist westerns that attempted to treat the Indians with sympathy and intelligence. The film was directed by Delmer Daves for 20th Century Fox.

Stewart plays Tom Jefford, a former army scout who has turned prospector in 1870. He nurses a wounded Apache boy back to health and decides to learn the Apache language to see if he can help bring about a peaceful end to the ten-year conflict that has raged in the territory. He wins the trust of the Apache Chief Cochise (Jeff Chandler) and falls in love with an Indian girl Sonseeaharay (the sixteen-year-old Debra Paget). With the Chief's permission he marries her and settles down to live with her in the Indian village. The new peace is interrupted by renegade elements from both sides. Sonseeaharay is killed in an attack upon Cochise's people, mistaken retaliation for the death of some whites. Stewart gives a fine dis-

*Below:* The poster for *It's a Wonderful Life* (1946) effectively captures its optimistic charm. Although the poster is color, the film is in fact a black and white classic of American film history. The poster shows the final scene from the movie, where George realizes how much he is loved by everyone in Bedford Falls.

LIBERTY FILMS INC.

presents FRANK CAPRA'S

"It's a Wonderful Life"

starring JAMES STEWART and DONNA REED

Distributed by RKO Radio Pictures Inc.

Copyright 1946 RKO Radio Pictures Inc. Country of Origin U.S.A.

play of raw emotion when he kills a captive from the band who shot his wife and wants to lead the Apaches in an attack upon the whites in order to avenge her death, but Cochise calms him by reminding him that the government had no part in the killing and that more violence will not ease his pain. *Broken Arrow* is an interesting, very genuine film which treats the Apache culture with respect; several hundred Apaches were used as extras in the movie, and the use of location shooting in the Coconino mountains helped the picture a greal deal visually. It was not universally loved by critics, however, some of whom pointed out that Debra Paget made an unconvincing Indian squaw, while some had their doubts about James Stewart the westerner. How wrong they were.

*Opposite:* Stewart puts a protective arm around Shelley Winters in *Winchester 73*. Winters brings out the tender side of the brutalized manhunter Stewart plays in the film.

*Below:* Stewart filmed his Broadway role of the bumbling, boozy Elwood P Dowd in *Harvey* (1951). Here he is in discussion with the phantom, six-foot white rabbit.

In *Winchester 73*, Stewart plays an even tougher, more abrasive character. The rifle of the title is a weapon of such precision that it cannot be sold but has to be won in competition. The film follows the much prized rifle as it passes from hand to hand, and the bitter feud between Lin McAdam (Stewart) and Dutch Henry Brown (Steven McNally), the man who shot and killed McAdam's father. We only learn that the two adversaries are brothers when the action culminates in a shootout on a rocky mountain outcrop. McAdam kills Brown after a hard fight, which is cleverly shot by Mann and his cinematographer William Daniels. Stewart's portrayal of McAdam is quite magnificent – he gives us a fully rounded characterization of an obsessed, deeply angry man. He is thoughtful and charming to a charming woman traveler (Shelley Winters) but also wholly convincing when he shows us McAdam's merciless side in the scene where he viciously twists an outlaw's arms behind his back and slams his head down on a table in an effort to extract information from him. This must have been quite a shock to audiences used to the gentle, smiling Stewart. The actor gives a sparse, pared-down performance – the usual hesitant charm and slow delivery are absent from his elliptical, sardonic McAdam.

*Harvey* was a return to a much gentler style of acting. The film was kept back by Universal as a Christmas treat for 1951; the studio had paid a small fortune for the rights to Mary Chase's play, in which Stewart had starred on Broadway for seven weeks in the summer of 1947. Both play and film became one of Stewart's best loved projects. It must be an odd feeling to know you will be forever identified as the bumbling boozy friend of an imaginary 6ft rabbit but Stewart has no complaints:

Wherever I go I'm always asked about Harvey, about how he is and where he is. At first I thought it was a joke but then I could see people were serious. So I just say that he's home with a cold and that I'll pass along the regards. Harvey's had a big effect on my life.

The film version, directed by Henry Koster, was nominated for Best Picture, Best Actor and Best Supporting Actress; the one statuette the film did win was for Josephine Hull's portrayal of Veta Louise. Stewart is completely convincing as Elwood P Dowd, a crumpled, gentle figure with a dreamy smile who roams around town with his best friend Harvey. They like to spend their time just chatting and getting to know people. Elwood has taken his mother's advice to be 'oh so smart or oh so pleasant' to heart; as he recalls, 'for years I was

oh so smart but now I recommend pleasant.'
Dowd is in his early forties and is a Capra-type
hero who has failed to deal with reality and so
has retreated into his fantasy life with Harvey,
his crutch and companion. The question the
story raises is who is the happier, the deluded
Elwood or his socialite sister Veta Louise, who
is embarrassed by her brother and fears he will
scare off her daughter's suitors. Critics and
public alike were pleased with the latest version of the Stewart persona but the film failed
to recoup its costs.

On May 7, 1951 Gloria Stewart gave birth to
twin daughters, Judy and Kelly. She had a difficult time with the birth and Stewart refused to
leave her bedside until she had recovered.
When she was well enough to go home he
came to collect her, but was in such a state of
excitement that he left her sitting at the bottom of the elevator and drove off without her.
Mrs Stewart was used to her husband's absent-
mindedness and calmly told the hospital staff
that Jimmy would ring as soon as he remembered his mistake; sure enough the phone soon
rang. Stewart has said of his forgetfulness: 'I'm
very guilty of daydreaming. Just can't seem to
keep my mind on anything.'

Stewart's next important film was *Bend of the
River*, his second western with director
Anthony Mann. He plays Glyn McLyntock, a
former border raider who is trying to make a
new life for himself. He is hired to guide a band
of pilgrims into the upper Snake River
country, where the group plans to establish a
farming community. He keeps his past hidden
from the farmers and their leader Jeremy Baile
(Jay C Flippen) who believes men cannot re-
form: 'When an apple's rotten there's nothing
you can do except throw it away.' Arthur Kennedy plays Emerson Cole, a truly bad apple and
former comrade of McLyntock's from his raid-
ing days. They meet up again when McLyntock saves Cole from a near lynching.

At first the two men work well together and
see off a band of Indians who try to approach
the wagon train at night. Cole does not believe
they will be forgiven their past wrongs and
soon reveals that he has not changed at all.
Cole and McLyntock undertake to liberate
supplies bought by Baile – the treacherous
merchant who sold them has double crossed
him. Cole wants to sell the goods to miners in a
nearby boom town who would pay handsomely
for them. He represents the pragmatic side of
the western character and the bad old days of
each man for himself. Cole and McLyntock
win the shoot-out with the merchant and his
men but Cole highjacks the goods high up in
the mountains. He stops the packers from
shooting McLyntock but leaves him alone to
die after beating him up in a savage fight.
There follows a superb moment, with Stewart
silhouetted against the blue sky and distant
peaks as he vows to Cole:

**Left:** James Stewart and family relax together in June 1951. From the left, Ronald (Gloria Stewart's six-year-old son), Gloria with Kelly on her lap, her four-year-old son Michael, and Kelly's twin sister Judy held by her father.

**Below:** Former comrades Stewart and Arthur Kennedy fight it out in the final scene of *Bend of the River* (1952).

You'll be seeing me, every time you look back in the darkness and you bed down for the night, you'll wonder if I'm there, and one day I will be. You'll be seeing me.

McLyntock recovers and his resolve to find Cole is as determined as his words. He tracks him down and Cole dies in the ensuing fight in a river – his body is washed downstream in a symbolic purging of Stewart's past.

*Bend of the River* is a great western with superb use of landscape, a feature of all the Stewart/Mann westerns. Borden Chase's writing has a rare clarity and Stewart and Kennedy are excellent as the men on whom the script's moral objective is so effectively focused. The financial success of the film left director and star free to go on working together – their next film was *The Naked Spur*, (1952) another Borden Chase script. Many film buffs regard this as their finest film together. It is a most unusual western, dealing as it does with only five characters and the interplay and psychological undercurrents between them. Stewart gives yet another fine performance as Howard Kemp, a bounty hunter who has been forced out of human society and is desperate to get back in. He needs money to buy back the land he lost while he was away fighting in the Civil War; he had entrusted it to his fiancée who betrayed him by selling it. Only the recovery of this land will enable Kemp to forgive himself his stupidity and regain his former humanity

**Left:** Janet Leigh tends to a wounded Stewart in *The Naked Spur* (1952), an unusual western and perhaps the best of the films Stewart made with Anthony Mann. It was certainly one of Stewart's greatest performances.

**Opposite:** Stewart looking remarkably like the much loved Glenn Miller in *The Glenn Miller Story* (1954). This was Stewart's fifth film with director Anthony Mann and the most popular film Stewart ever made. His imitation of Miller was so good that many people thought it was Stewart playing on the soundtrack. In fact, his attempts to learn to play the trombone were something of a comic disaster.

**Below:** Stewart pictured with the singer Frances Langford, who played herself in *The Glenn Miller Story.*

and compassion. He is a good man turned angry and defiant in the face of the wrongdoing of others – a role Stewart was particularly adept at playing.

Posing as a sheriff, Kemp goes to Colorado to hunt down escaped killer Ben Vandergoat (Robert Ryan), a man whose capture dead or alive can earn him $5000. He meets up with an old prospector (Millard Mitchell) and a dishonorably discharged army lieutenant (Ralph Meeker), who agree to help him in his quest, but demand a share of any money when they find out he is a bounty hunter. They capture Vandergoat on his way to California with a young woman, Lina (Janet Leigh), who clings to him because he was a friend of her dead father. Vandergoat slyly exploits the differences between the three men and uses Lina as a sexual ploy between Kemp and the ex-soldier. Vandergoat manages to escape but is shot and killed by Kemp, whose life is saved by Lina when she distracts Vandergoat just as he is about to take aim at Kemp. She has fallen in love with him after hearing him murmer in his sleep and reveal the reasons why he appears to be so hard-hearted.

Kemp hauls Vandergoat's body out of the raging torrent into which he fell when he was shot. As he thumps the corpse on to a slab of rock he is clearly in torment, hysterically insisting to Lina that he must hand in the body for the reward – 'I'm taking him back, I swear it.' But his obsessional drive for revenge is futile now he has Lina's love. Seeking justice against fate he had been alone and friendless but he can now free himself of the pain of the past and move on to a better future. As he picks up a shovel to bury Vandergoat he smiles at Lina and asks: 'Still wanna go to California?' At one point Kemp is shot in the leg by Ralph Meeker's soldier and, as in *Bend of the River*,

Stewart's rendering of the pain and physical suffering of a basically good man is intensely real and moving. It is without question one of Stewart's greatest performances but one which sadly did not gain him an Academy Award nomination.

*The Naked Spur* was followed by two more Stewart/Mann collaborations: *Thunder Bay* (1953), a western-style, very commercial drama about drilling for oil, and the hugely popular *The Glenn Miller Story* (1954). A film biography about Glenn Miller would have had to misfire pretty badly to disappoint at the box office, and in the able hands of Stewart and

Mann it is an enjoyable, likeable portrait. Again Stewart plays a man with a mission. Glenn Miller searched for years to find that special sound which he stumbled on quite by accident. June Allyson plays Miller's wife Helen; she was so keen to work again with Stewart that she did not even bother to read the script before accepting the part. Helen does not allow Miller to forget his musical dream and waste his talent playing the trombone in other people's bands. She uses her savings to set him up in the Glenn Miller Band, where he can play his special arrangements his way. Stewart exhibits his famous stubborn

**Left:** Stewart portrays Miller making one of his famous BBC recordings during the Second World War. The film satisfactorily reproduced the Miller sound, part of the US renaissance of jazz in the form of big-band swing in the 1930s.

streak to good effect and skilfully points up the shyness beneath Miller's comic self-assurance, especially in the scenes where he courts Helen. The film avoids mawkish sentimentality and sticks closely to the facts of Miller's life. His tragic death at the age of forty when his plane disappeared over the English Channel on a flight to Paris is cleverly underplayed.

Stewart did not play the trombone in the film but mimicked Miller's hand and lip movements so well that many people thought it was Stewart on the soundtrack. Joe Yuki dubbed Stewart's playing, but not before the actor had had a go himself. He was assigned a coach,

who found the noise emitted by Stewart's trombone so unbearable that he threatened to quit. 'But I talked him into staying,' explains Stewart, 'and we solved the problem. I plugged up the mouthpiece on my trombone so that it was impossible for me to make a sound – it was certainly cheating but it was the only way.' *The Glenn Miller Story* is the most popular film in which James Stewart starred. This massively successful musical, and his next release, *Rear Window*, put Stewart into the top ten box office attractions of 1954. His career had reached its peak and there were still plenty of good things to come.

**Left:** Stewart says goodbye to Mrs Miller (June Allyson) and their children in the scene where Miller departs for England.

# Chapter 5
# FILMING WITH HITCHCOCK AND FORD 1955-

*R*ope had not been the best of beginnings for Hitchcock and Stewart's film partnership but their second film, *Rear Window*, is one of the finest in their respective careers. As in *Vertigo* and *The Man Who Knew Too Much*, Stewart is quite excellent in the role of an ordinary man forced to react to extraordinary circumstances. L B 'Jeff' Jeffries is used to traveling the world in his job as an ace magazine photographer. A broken leg in plaster leaves him confined to a wheelchair

*Below:* A telling shot from *Rear Window*, the classic Hitchcock thriller released in 1954. Stewart plays action man Jeff who is forced to watch the world from his wheelchair after an accident.

and bored, until he discovers the fun to be had in spying on the people in the Manhattan apartment building opposite his. What he does not expect to discover is that a salesman, Mr Thorswald (Raymond Burr), has murdered his wife and looks set to get clean away with it; only Stewart has noticed anything amiss and he fails to convince his detective friend (Wendell Corey) that there is anything wrong. Grace Kelly plays Jeff's girlfriend, the lovely fashion designer Lisa Fremondt, and Thelma Ritter is the insurance nurse Stella, the sensible counterpoint to the drama.

Stella does her best to encourage Jeff to marry the 'perfect' Lisa but he is worried about being tied down and protests to Lisa that their lifestyles are too different, telling her 'those high heels – they'll be great in the jungle.' Lisa and Stella are persuaded that Jeff's suspicions about Thorswald are justified and Lisa seizes the chance to be Jeff's legs and goes over to the murder apartment to investigate. But Thorswald returns to catch her and she has to pretend to be a thief. A frantic Jeff is watching all this through his binoculars and rings the police who arrive in time to save Lisa and she is taken away to jail. Stella goes to bail her out, leaving Jeff alone and vulnerable in his apartment. Suddenly the watcher is confronted by the watched when Thorswald invades Jeff's apartment intent on killing him. We only see Raymond Burr's eyes glinting in the darkness as he approaches Stewart, helpless in his wheelchair. Jeff desperately attempts to disarm the killer by blinding him with the flashbulb of his camera. The police arrive in the nick of time but not before Jeff falls from his balcony window as he struggles with Thorswald, breaking his other leg.

*Rear Window* is a very fine, unusual thriller and is an interesting comment on the nature of voyeurism, an activity which Hitchcock believed was very close to the art of cinema itself. The relationship between the middle-aged photographer and his gorgeous girlfriend, who just can't resist taking on the role of sexual predator to the enfeebled Stewart, is beautifully played. Stewart loved working with Grace Kelly and was particularly taken with her playing in the scene where she steals into the killer's apartment – 'I think she did an amazing job as my girlfriend who has to do my dirty work.' MGM had plans to put Kelly and Stewart in a second film, *Designing Women*, but Kelly stopped the show when she announced she was marrying Prince Rainier of Monaco.

Stewart's next two films reunited him with Anthony Mann – their fourth western *The Far Country* (1955) and *Strategic Air Command* (1955), a worthy but dull attempt to boost the morale of the SAC (Stewart was himself an officer in the Air Force Reserve at the time).

There is no revenge motif in *The Far Country* but Stewart's character, the Wyoming wrangler Jeff Webster, is not too far removed from Lyn McAdam and Glyn McLyntock and shares their qualities of stubborness and obstinate independence. Webster is another who has been mistreated by his fellow man – his motto is now 'I take care of me' – but he retains an essential goodness of character which prevails in the end. In his script (his third for Stewart), Borden Chase enlarges upon the theme of a man having to forget his personal pain to work for the good of the community. By the end of the picture Webster has single-handedly revived the idea of setting up a proper community among the townspeople of Skagway, Alaska. *The Far Country* is the most conventional of the Stewart/Mann westerns, but the quality script, use of Technicolor footage shot on location in the Canadian Rockies, and the breathtakingly dramatic scenery itself, set the movie apart from others with similarly redemptive plot lines.

Anthony Mann had long cherished the idea of making a western inspired by the theme of Shakespeare's *King Lear*; when he came to the end of a seven-year contract with Universal, he was finally able to make *The Man From Laramie*. Stewart again took up the role of hero

*Below:* Stewart loved working with the beautiful Grace Kelly, who was perfectly cast as his witty, determined girlfriend in *Rear Window*.

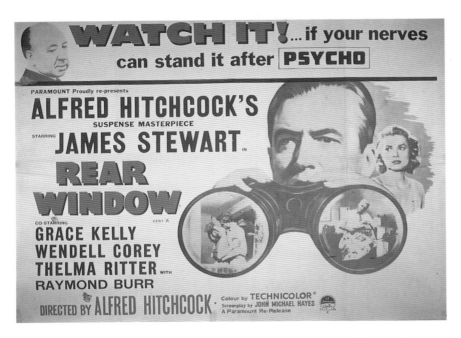

as avenger in playing Bill Lockhart, the man from Laramie, who states 'I can't rightly say any place is my home.' We gradually learn that he was an army captain at Fort Laramie and is now seeking the gunrunners who sold weapons to the Indians who killed his brother, a young army officer. Wallace Ford plays the half-Indian old timer who volunteers to help the dogged Lockhart in his quest. Lockhart is an emotionally burdened, suffering hero, deeply reticent and only capable of expressing his rage. Posing as a sheriff, he rides into New Mexico in persuit of his goal and arrives at Coronado, a country town controled by the rich and powerful Alex Waggoman (Donald Crisp). On a trip out of town to collect more merchandise, Lockhart is brutally attacked by Waggoman's weak, spoilt, psychopathic son Dave (Alex Nichol). He is lassooed and dragged through a fire, his wagons burnt and his mules shot, all purely for the amusement of Dave. Vic Hanboro (Arthur Kennedy), Waggoman's foreman and foster son, intervenes to stop Dave killing Lockhart. When he returns to Coronado, Lockhart is paid financial compensation by Waggoman and told to get out of town, but stays out of affection for Waggoman's niece Barbara and because a friendly woman rancher has offered him a job.

Hanboro is furious when he finds out Waggoman has named Dave as his sole heir, and his disgust for his brother deepens when he sees him shoot Lockhart in the hand while two of his men hold him down. This was rare and brutal violence for 1955 and Stewart's anguished cry of 'You scum!' as the bullet is fired point-blank into his hand still has the power to shock. Lockhart recovers and pursues his investigation but it is Waggoman who discovers the truth – Dave and Hanboro sold the guns to the Indians in an act of rebellion against their father. Waggoman falls off a cliff during a confrontation with Dave, but before he dies he tells Lockhart all he knows. Dave is then killed by Hanboro, who is hunted down by Lockhart. Stewart rides silhouetted against the night sky as he tracks down his old nemesis Arthur Kennedy. When he finds him they push a wagon full of more guns for the Indians over the edge

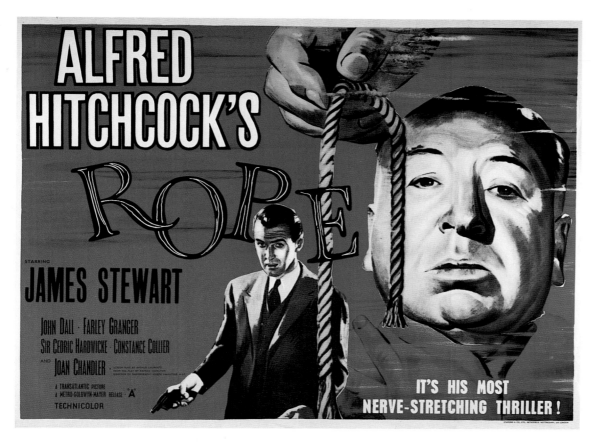

of a hill. Lockhart's breath is heavy with hatred as he tells Hanboro: 'I came a thousand miles to kill you. I'm not going to rush it – I've waited a long time for this.' But he finds he can't kill the unarmed man; he gasps 'Get away from me' at a grateful Hanboro and so retains his heroic status.

With *The Man From Laramie*, Stewart and Mann's partnership ended on a fittingly high note. Mann went on to direct one more excellent western, *Man of the West*, and then worked on the lavish productions of *El Cid*, *The Fall of the Roman Empire*, and *The Heroes of Telmark*. He and Stewart fell out over the

*Left:* A reflective scene from *The Man From Laramie* (1955), Stewart's last film with Anthony Mann. The high standard of their work together was certainly maintained in this fine western, which was considered very brutal at the time.

making of *Night Passage*, a film Mann had been scheduled to direct; he was unhappy about the script and backed away from it. They resumed their friendship before Mann's death from a heart attack in 1967 at the age of 61, but sadly never had the chance to work together again. Mann found in Stewart the perfect actor to transmit his ideas about the nature of the western character. He always admired Stewart's willingness to submit himself to physical hardship and once paid his friend the following tribute, describing Stewart as a man:

Who's devoted his whole life to acting and who's quite brilliant at what he does. He's very skilful and, once you start going with him, he's marvelous to work with, because he's always there, he's always anxious, he wants to be great.

One very important and productive partnership was at an end, but Stewart still had the great Hitchcock to work with in two more films. In *The Man Who Knew Too Much*, Stewart gives a very believable rendition of a successful man whose well ordered life is suddenly plunged into a crisis when his son is kidnapped while his wife (Doris Day) and he are on holiday in Morocco. The boy is taken to

prevent the Stewart character (Dr Ben McKenna) revealing what he has learnt about an espionage plot to murder a visiting diplomat in London. McKenna arrives at the Albert Hall just in time to foil the murder. He knows that the assassin's cue will be the clashing of cymbals in the orchestra's playing of *Storm Clouds Cantata*, and Doris Day's scream at the sight of a gun appearing through the curtains startles the murderer, who is chased to his death falling from a box high in the stalls. The film's considerable commercial success was helped along by Doris Day's number one hit single 'Que Sera', which was taken from the movie. It is not a Hitchcock film held in great esteem by his many admirers, and the picture was criticized as not measuring up to the original version, made by Hitchcock in 1934. But Paramount had demanded a family-oriented drama as well as a suspenseful yarn and that is what they got.

*The Man Who Knew Too Much* was Stewart's eighth box office hit in a row, a run which could not long continue and in fact crashed in spectacular style with *The Spirit of St Louis*, which Jack Warner termed 'the most disastrous film we ever made.' It was a project very dear to Stewart's heart, but failed to overcome several inherent problems: at 48 Stewart was much too old to play the 25-year-old Charles Lindbergh; not enough people knew the name of the plane in which he made his historic solo Atlantic flight; and although Billy Wilder was a very great director, he was the wrong choice for this film. The picture cost $6 million to make, an enormous sum for 1957, when the film was finally released, and although it is very entertaining and absorbing it failed miserably at the box office.

Stewart's bad luck continued with *Night Passage*, probably the least of his westerns in the 1950s, but Hitchcock was on hand to repair any damage done to Stewart's career by these last two flops, and in offering Stewart the lead role in *Vertigo* he did so in magnificent style. *Vertigo* is a film which bears watching again and again and it gave Stewart a fantastic role – the haunted, obsessive policeman with a disastrous fear of heights. This dark tale of love is a quite exceptional film for 1958 and the passing of time has only enhanced its reputation. It is a film atypical of Hitchcock: suspense takes second place to psychology, and it goes against the grain of its genre – the hero is neurotic and deeply unhappy, the heroine ends up dead (twice), and the villain literally gets away with murder. Scottie Ferguson (Stewart) is a retired policeman and something of a loner – 'some people prefer it that way' – although he was once engaged at college to the very sensible Midge (Barbara Bel Geddes), who still adores him. He retired from the police service after a rooftop chase, in which a colleague died, left him with a crip-

*Below:* Stewart apprehensively undertakes an act of derring do in his role as *The Man Who Knew Too Much* (1956). His third film with Alfred Hitchcock was their least successful artistically but a big hit commercially.

pling fear of heights. He sets himself up as a private detective and is hired by an old school friend, Gavin Estler, who believes his wife Madeline (Kim Novak) is possessed by her grandmother Carlotta, who committed suicide many years earlier. 'Do you believe that someone out of the past, someone dead, can enter and take possession of someone living?' Estler asks Scottie, who himself becomes the tragic victim of such a phenomenon. Scottie trails the enigmatic, beautiful Madeline and is intrigued by her strange trancelike behavior, which culminates in a suicide bid when she jumps into the bay from the San Francisco Golden Gate bridge. Scottie saves her and takes her back to his apartment where he undresses her and puts her to bed. By the time she wakes up the next morning he is completely besotted with her, saying: 'I'm responsible for you now. You know the Chinese say that once you've saved a person's life, you're responsible for it for ever. So you're committed.'

He takes her to the old Spanish mission at San Juan Batista about which she recurrently dreams, and as soon as they arrive there she rushes up the belltower steps and throws herself off the top. Scottie tries to follow her but his vertigo impedes him and he has to watch in horror as she plunges past him to her death on the ground below. The coroner at the inquest criticizes Scottie and this, combined with the loss of his love, precipitates a nervous breakdown and a spell in a sanitorium, where a loving Midge helps to nurse him back to health. Time passes and is beginning to heal Scottie when he stumbles across a girl in the street who looks exactly like Madeline. She is Judy Barton (Kim Novak again), a dark-haired shop assistant who is a more ordinary version of the beautiful Madeline. Scottie falls in love again, without realizing that Judy and Madeline are the same woman. Hitchcock reveals only to the audience that Judy was hired by Estler to masquerade as his wife, so that his real wife could be killed and her body thrown off the belltower when she was already dead. There is a terrible desperation in the scene where Scottie begs Judy to change her looks to make her a replica of Madeline. It is a macabre, very Hitchcockian spectacle, which the director referred to as having the 'compulsion of a striptease in reverse.' Judy responds to Scottie and grows to love him and to regret her part in the terrible deception. She is distressed to see he has no real interest in her but is still lost in his love for Madeline.

When Judy inadvertently gives away her secret, Scottie has no mercy in his pain and rage. He forces her to through the details of the murder plot so he 'can be free of the past and have a second chance,' but this cannot happen. He takes Judy back to the belltower and is so angry as he forces her up the steps that his vertigo disappears. He makes her stand at the

edge of the tower platform to frighten more of the truth out of her. He embraces and kisses her, but loses her in the same instant when she is startled by a black shadow emerging from the shadows (actually a nun) and falls to her death. We see a final, haunting image of Stewart, arms helplessly outstretched, looking down on the broken body of the woman he has loved and lost twice.

The blackness of the story clearly appealed to Alfred Hitchcock, one can almost see his eyes smiling as he observed: 'He (Scottie) wants to go to bed with a dead woman. He is indulging in a form of necrophilia.' Stewart gave one of his very greatest performances in *Vertigo* – perhaps his finest ever, it is certainly a remarkable piece of acting. It is his portrayal of a disturbed man that overcomes the absurdities and weaknesses of the plot. Hitchcock had originally wanted Vera Miles for the role of Madeline but Paramount persuaded him to use Kim Novak and her passive, remote beauty was perfect for the film. As Stewart observed, 'It worked. It was there. We had "the chemistry".' Novak has spoken of her respect for Stewart and her words express what many Americans felt about Stewart's place in their affections: 'He was what I wanted my America

*Above:* A near-deranged Stewart forces a confession from Kim Novak in the magnificent *Vertigo* (1958), Stewart's last film with Hitchcock.

a role to be played. Stewart took on a very major role when he decided to play Paul Biegler, small-town Chicago defence lawyer. He had a huge amount of dialogue to learn as he was on screen for every scene of the two-and-a-half-hour picture, leaving him only one free afternoon during the eight weeks of shooting.

The role was dangerous for his reputation as the clean-cut American hero, as the film's plot centers on a rape and this subjectmatter had before never been dealt with so openly and in such clinical detail. Some of Stewart's older fans wrote letters of protest and Alex Stewart demanded to know why his son was appearing in 'that dirty picture.' But a man as astute and intelligent as James Stewart would never turn down a role as good as Paul Biegler, the down-at-heel attorney who wins a very tough case against the odds. Biegler is asked to defend army lieutenant Frederick Mannion (Ben Gazarra) who is accused of murdering the bartender whom he alleges raped his wife (Lee Remick). Mannion is an unpleasant character but as Biegler's acerbic secretary (Eve Arden) points out, 'You don't have to love him – just defend him!' The prosecution, who have hired a sharp-talking, high-powered lawyer from out of town (George C Scott), are convinced they are on to a sure thing but Biegler uses his excellent legal brain to turn things around. He is determined that Mannion should be given a fair trial but learns a lesson in human nature at the end of the picture, when Mannion and his wife skip town without paying their bill. The film is a realistic depiction of a trial in which there is no black and white solution; the audience has to make up its own mind, just like the jury. The *New York Times* congratulated Stewart on his performance:

Slowly and subtly he presents us a warm, clever, adroit and complex man and, most particularly, a portrait of a trial lawyer in action which will be difficult for anyone to surpass.

It is a sad fact that James Stewart and John Ford did not work together until both their careers were drawing to a close. Stewart became the last major star to work with the great director when he signed to appear in *Two Rode Together* before Ford had even fully agreed to direct it. He plays his first wholly corrupt, morally questionable character in this cynical western, which has a similar theme to Ford's great 1956 western *The Searchers*. Richard Widmark co-stars as the idealistic soldier who accompanies Stewart's Guthrie McCabe in the quest to liberate prisoners held by Commanchees. McCabe is a selfish man whose creed through the film is 'What's in it for me?' – a long way from the high moral fervor of Jefferson Smith. Ford is reputed to have lost interest in *Two Rode Together*. He made only two more westerns but he cast James Stewart in both of them.

to represent – pride, dignity and honor in a place where people were capable of deception.'

Stewart's career stumbled after *Vertigo* and he found it hard to maintain such a high quality of work, but he made one more film worthy of his great talent before the decade ended, *Anatomy of a Murder*. The New York film critics named him their choice as Best Actor and he would surely have won the Academy Award for which he was nominated had *Ben Hur* not swept the board, picking up ten Oscars including Best Actor for Charlton Heston. *Anatomy of a Murder* was based on Robert Traver's best selling novel and was directed by Otto Preminger who, unlike Hitchcock, had a reputation for knowing exactly how he wanted

Stewart and Ford's second western together, *The Man Who Shot Liberty Valance*, is their best and most important film. The film contains the famous line 'When the legend becomes fact, print the legend,' and takes that line as its premise in its examination of how myth often overtook fact in the forging of the West. Stewart jumped at the chance to make his first film with John Wayne in what is really Wayne's film. Both actors were too old for their roles as young men of ambition in the West but with a little make-up and their very special appeal, nobody cared. Stewart's role was something of a reprisal of the idealism and integrity of Senator Jefferson Smith but in *Liberty Valance* the lawmaker has grown older and much wiser.

The story begins with a young lawyer, Ranson Stoddard (James Stewart) riding into the town of Shinbone on the stagecoach; just before he gets there he is whipped and badly beaten up by Liberty Valance (Lee Marvin) and his band of roughnecks. He is found by Tom Doniphon (John Wayne), a small-time cattleman and the only man in Shinbone Liberty Valance can't bully or intimidate. Stoddard is nursed back to health by Doniphon and his girlfriend Hallie (Vera Miles) whose Swedish parents run a restaurant in town. Doniphon is amused by Stoddard's desire to bring the brutal, boastful Valance to justice, knowing all too well that Valance is a protected man because he is a hireling of the powerful ranchers who oppose statehood for the territory. The town has no effective system of justice because the weak marshall is understandably afraid of Valance.

A town with no law has no need for lawyers, so Stoddard goes to work for Hallie's parents as a waiter and dishwasher; Hallie grows increasingly fond of Stoddard, who teaches her and some others in the town to read and write. Stoddard has an admirable enthusiasm for justice and liberty but no practical means with which to enforce his ideals. He embodies the new modernism of the East and insists that it is the West, not he, who must change. He continues to wear drab, Eastern-style suits and clashes with Doniphon who believes the old ways and his method of doing things will prevail. Doniphon tells Stoddard that the only way to deal with a man like Valance is to shoot him but Stoddard answers: 'I don't want to kill him. I want to put him in jail.' He does not at first carry a gun but a humiliating encounter in a restaurant with Valance changes his mind and he begins to practise in secret with a revolver. This worries Hallie, who asks Doniphon to help him, but he instead deliberately humiliates Stoddard in a shooting lesson.

With the help of the local newspaper editor, Stoddard makes it known that he is out to bring law and order to Shinbone, and starts to organize the local people to use their vote in

*Left:* Kim Novak plays two roles in *Vertigo*, the beautiful, mysterious Madeline and the more ordinary Judy, a shop girl who is Madeline's double. Here she is seen as Judy with Stewart, whose character does not yet know that the two women are really one and the same.

favor of statehood. This upsets the cattle barons and they hire Valance to take care of the upstart lawyer, who refuses to back away from the coming confrontation. He faces Valance in a darkened street at night and wins the shootout, much to his and everyone else's surprise. The real surprise comes when we learn that it was Doniphon who killed Valance, by targeting him from the shadows, an act of great unselfishness as he is still in love with Hallie, whom he wants to marry. His nobility makes Stoddard the town hero and he is nominated for government office, but feels that he cannot except because he has killed a

*Below:* Stewart, in much lighter mood, relaxes on the beach in *Mr Hobbs Takes a Vacation* (1962), the first of a series of popular domestic comedies he made in the early 1960s.

*Right:* Stewart attempts to stop George C Scott from intimidating his witness (Lee Remick) during the trial in *Anatomy of a Murder* (1959). Remick plays a woman whose husband has been accused of the murder of a bartender who allegedly raped her. Based on a highly detailed courtroom bestseller, the film featured a real-life judge as the trial judge.

man. But Doniphon, a man of good sense and realism, dispels his friend's illusions and reveals that he shot Valance, telling Stoddard that if he wants to do some good for Hallie and Shinbone then he should accept the great chance he is offered. So Stoddard goes along with the pretence and builds upon it to become a successful senator in Washington, responsible for bringing the territory into statehood.

The film starts with his return to Shinbone to attend the funeral of Tom Doniphon, who has died a bachelor, alone and poor. Stoddard decides to end the lie that has brought him so much and tells the true story to a journalist. He is amazed that the reporter rejects the scoop with the words: 'As our late and great editor used to say, "It ain't news. This is the West. When the legend becomes fact, print the legend".' It is a great pity that Ford, Stewart and Wayne waited for so long before working together as *Liberty Valance* is such a good film, as well as a rare introspective look by Ford into the legend of the West and his own part in bringing that legend to life in the imagination of so many. Wayne and Stewart play opposite sides of the same coin – the virile individualist, and the idealist who learns the value of pragmatism. Stewart is particularly splendid in the early scenes, where he splutters with indignation at Lee Marvin's swaggering brutality.

Stewart made thirteen films in the 1960s, eight of them westerns. One of these, *Shenandoah*, is his second outstanding film of that decade and by far the best of his four films with director Andrew McClaglen. The picture is a forceful and eloquent ant-war drama, set in 1853. Stewart plays a Virginian farmer, a fiercely independent patriarch, who stoutly defends his right to ignore the Civil War that is being fought all around him: 'This war is not mine and I take no note of it,' he tells the Confederate officer who comes to the farm demanding to know why his sons have not enlisted. Charlie, the only name Stewart is given in the film, has six sons and one daughter and his youngest, known as Boy, is particularly dear to him, because it was in giving him life that his beloved wife Martha lost hers. Charlie gives his sons the choice but they all want to stay on the farm. The war is a persistent enemy, however, and the family's life is disrupted when Charlie's precious Boy is seized by Union soldiers. Now Charlie goes to war on the conflict itself, vowing: 'Now it concerns me . . . I don't know how these people dare take a son of mine – when I catch up with them it's going to be a horrible sight to behold.'

Charlie even insists on a place being laid for Boy at the table after he has been taken. He is a man incapable of compromise. The whole family is involved in the search for the youngest son and three of them die as a result. They do not manage to find Boy who finds his own way home, limping up the aisle as the family attend church and walking straight into the strong, loving arms of his father. Stewart is magnificent in his role as the stubborn, proud, big-hearted pacifist who undergoes a profound change and learns that he cannot always control the events that affect his life. He is the last

**Left:** Stewart lies injured after a beating from Lee Marvin who played the villain in *The Man Who Shot Liberty Valance*. John Wayne stands by as Vera Miles attends to Stewart.

**Below:** A grimly determined Stewart leads his family in the hunt for his youngest son in the 1965 western *Shenandoah*.

in a long line of Stewart's moral, deeply principled men who are ferocious when pushed. When Charlie speaks his piece after failing to find his son – 'Somehow I just had to try . . . if we don't try, we don't do' – it could just as easily be the hero of so many other Stewart films speaking. *Shenandoah* gave Stewart the last part that was truly worthy of his great talents. *Newsweek* paid him the following compliment:

What Stewart himself achieves must be a source of some discouragement as well as instruction to the young unskilled actors working with him. He is far from young. His role of paterfamilias is more tired than his eyes. Yet Stewart compels belief with his strength and his simplicity.

To say Stewart's performance dominates the film is something of an understatement.

Stewart had had a constant companion in all his westerns since *Winchester 73*, a sorrel, part-Arab horse called Pie. He liked Pie so much he tried to buy him but the owner was too fond of him to sell. Pie was no ordinary horse in Stewart's eyes, as this affectionate anecodote reveals:

I got to know him like a friend. I actually believe that he understood about making pictures. I've run at a full gallop straight toward the camera and then had a lot of dialogue and he's sat absolutely still and never moved. He was smart as a whip. He knew when the camera would start rolling – when they did the slates. He knew that, because his ears came up and I could feel him under me get ready and he

*Right:* Stewart and Carroll Baker in a scene from *How the West Was Won* (1962).

*Far Right:* Stewart as attorney Jim Hawkins in the television series *Hawkins* in 1973.

*Below:* Jimmy Stewart joins in the celebrations at Chasen's restaurant in honor of the great Frank Capra, the director to whom he owed so much.

always moved . . . and the other horses didn't know what was going on, so he'd stand out.

Pie was scheduled to appear with Stewart in *The Cheyenne Social Club*, the 1970 comedy western about a humble old cowboy who un-

wittingly inherits a bordello. But Pie labored for breath in the high altitude of New Mexico and Stewart refused to use him. His co-star Henry Fonda was a talented artist and, knowing the great affection his friend had for the horse, he painted a picture of him in secret. Pie

died two days after Fonda presented Stewart with the painting, and in Stewart's words, '. . . it was a great loss. But I have Pie in our library and I consider him a friend.' Stewart and Fonda's friendship endured for 50 years, from their meeting as members of the University Players in 1932 until Fonda's death in 1982. They were political opposites – Fonda was a liberal Democrat and Stewart is a conservative Republican, but they did not let this spoil their relationship, coming to a very sensible arrangement, as Stewart explains – 'Hank and I never, never discussed politics.'

It was during the making of *The Cheyenne Social Club* that Stewart's stepson Ronald, a Marine Lieutenant, died eleven days before his 25th birthday in Vietnam. Stewart did not believe his son died in vain: 'His mother and I are proud that he served his country.' Stewart supported America's involvement in Vietnam and disagreed with those who saw the death of Ronald and the thousands like him as tragic: 'What's tragic is boys giving their lives without having a unified country behind him. That's what's tragic.'

Stewart made only one more western in the 1970s, a decade which saw the virtual demise of this great genre. *The Shootist* reunited him with his friend John Wayne and he was glad to be asked to play a small part in this elegy to the Great Westerner. By this time Stewart was rejecting nearly every part offered him, but the small role of doctor and old acquaintance who

***Above:*** Jimmy and Gloria arrive at the Gala Tribute to Stewart given by the Film Society of Lincoln Center, New York, in April 1990.

***Left:*** Stewart clasps his honorary Oscar at the Academy Awards ceremony in Los Angeles in March 1985. The award was presented to Stewart by another Hollywood great, Cary Grant, who spoke of Stewart as a man 'we all love and admire for his decency, his strength and his kindness.'

must tell Wayne he is dying of cancer (as indeed he was at the time) was much too good to pass up. Ably directed by Don Siegel, *The Shootist* is a poignant, special film – no story could have been more appropriate for Wayne's last movie. Wayne once said of Stewart: 'Whenever I'd get discouraged about the movie business, I'd think of him and thank my lucky stars that he was part of it.' When Wayne died in 1979, Stewart said simply: 'He was a fine man. A very fine man.' Since 1975 James Stewart has lived a life of virtual retirement, only making the occasion cameo appearance in films such as *Airport 77* and *The Big Sleep*, Michael Winner's dismal remake of the Bogart/Chandler classic; his last starring role was in *The Magic of Lassie* (1978) a revamp of *Lassie Come Home* with an ageing but all-star cast. Modern Hollywood has little space for its old-time legends; as Stewart says, 'There are less and less movie parts – let's face it – because of my age.' He is disenchanted with much of today's cinema:

The trouble is the movies they're making today are the wrong kind of movies, the seamy, depressing, hopeless, semi-pornographic things. At this point why should I fool around with stuff like that?'

The small screen reaped some benefit from this disillusionment. For a long time Stewart held out against his own TV show and was content to confine his appearances to guest spots on other people's shows. But NBC's offer of $35,000 a week tempted him to make a half hour situation comedy for their 1971-2 season. *The Jimmy Stewart Show* was very much built around the Stewart charisma and was criticized for being too dull and staid. Stewart accepted some of the responsibility for this; 'I had too much authority.' Much better was the Hawkins series of TV films in which Stewart played an elderly, wily, bachelor criminal lawyer, the kind of man his Paul Biegler in *Anatomy of a Murder* would have become 20 or so years on down the road. The series was well received and Stewart picked up the 1974 Golden Globe award for Best Actor.

Stewart's achievements in life have by no means been confined to his acting career. As well as his fine service record in the Second World War, Stewart served in the US Air Forces Reserve for two decades and attained the rank of Brigadier. He was awarded the Distinguished Service Medal, only the second time it had been awarded to a reserve officer. Stewart is an immensely patriotic man and is proud of his service in the armed forces: 'I spent twenty seven years in the military, and it meant a great deal to me in my life. I know that the principles and standards I learned made me a better citizen.'

Stewart has been blessed with a very happy marriage which has lasted more than 40 years. When Frank Capra asked him why he thought his partnership with Gloria had been so successful, a great rarity in Hollywood, Stewart

*Right:* Henry Fonda and James Stewart survey the delights of the bordello Stewart is surprised to learn he has inherited in *The Cheyenne Social Club* (1970).

replied: 'I guess it's that Gloria and I really like each other and we're not afraid to show it.' Gloria credits her husband as being 'much too normal to be an actor.' She says Jimmy has always 'shunned nightclubs and likes nothing better than to spend an evening at home.'

James Stewart has received all the praise and tributes due to him as one of the very greatest movie stars there has ever been and ever will be. In February 1980, the American Film Institute gave him its Life Achievement Award and in March 1985 Cary Grant presented his old friend with the Academy of Motion Pictures Arts and Sciences Special Oscar for his contribution to the film industry. Stewart is the last living male star to be numbered among the Hollywood Greats and so is to be treasured all the more. Cary Grant, Henry Fonda, John Wayne, Spencer Tracy, James Cagney, Humphrey Bogart and Gary Cooper are all gone, as Stewart is all too sadly aware. There have been many wonderful movie stars but very few have possessed Stewart's wide range and extraordinary depth of talent. The very name James Stewart is synonymous with the qualities he was able to portray so well on screeen –

honesty, decency and strength of character. It is a name which conjures up all that is best about what it means to be an American. He is so closely identified with his country that Stewart, a staunch Republican, could surely have run for President had he so wanted. This brings to mind a telling joke that went around Hollywood when the news broke that Ronald Reagan was going to do just that. The joke went something like – 'NO, NO, Jimmy Stewart for President. Ronald Reagan for his best friend.' (Reagan and Stewart, incidentally, are very old friends)

Stewart has spoken of how he would like to be remembered: ' . . . if they write "He gave people a lot of pleasure" on my epitaph I shall be very pleased. I've had many people tell me that they remember certain little things I did in pictures. I think it's wonderful to have been able to give people little pieces of pleasure they can remember.' There are so many words that one could use to express one's admiration for James Stewart but perhaps Prince Philip said it for all of us when he told Stewart on meeting him at a film premiere in London: 'Thankyou for being Jimmy Stewart.'

*Above:* Two old friends relax on the set of *The Cheyenne Social Club*, a gentle comedy western directed by Gene Kelly. Stewart and Fonda's friendship endured for 50 years, from their days in the University Players in the early 1930s to Fonda's death in 1982.

# Filmography

### 1934
*Art Trouble* DIR Ralph Staub, starring Harry Gribbon, Shemp Howard, Beatrice Blinn, Lenni Stengel

### 1935
*The Murder Man* DIR Tim Whelan, starring Spencer Tracy, Virginia Bruce, Lionel Atwill, Harry Stephens

### 1936
*Rose Marie* DIR W S Van Dyke II, starring Jeanette MacDonald, Nelson Eddy

*Next Time We Love* DIR Edward H. Griffith, starring Margaret Sullavan, Ray Milland, Grant Mitchell

*Wife Versus Secretary* DIR Clarence Brown, starring Clark Gable, Jean Harlow, Myrna Loy

*Important News* DIR Edwin Laurence, starring Chic Sale

*Small Town Girl* DIR William A Wellman, starring Janet Gaynor, Robert Taylor, Binnie Barnes, Lewis Stone

*Speed* DIR Edwin L Marin, starring Wendy Barrie, Una Merkel, Weldon Heyburn, Ted Healy

*The Gorgeous Hussy* DIR Clarence Brown, starring Joan Crawford, Robert Taylor, Lionel Barrymore, Franchot Tone, Melvyn Douglas, Louis Calhern

*Born to Dance* DIR Roy Del Ruth, starring Eleanor Powell, Virginia Bruce, Una Merkel, Sid Silvers

*After the Thin Man* DIR W S Van Dyke II, starring William Powell, Myrna Loy, Elissa Landi

### 1937
*Seventh Heaven* DIR Henry King, starring Simone Simon, Jean Hersholt, Gregory Ratoff

*The Last Gangster* DIR Edward Ludwig, starring Edward G Robinson, Rose Stradner, Lionel Stander

*Navy Blue and Gold* DIR Sam Wood, starring Robert Taylor, Lionel Barrymore

### 1938
*Of Human Hearts* DIR Clarence Brown, starring Walter Huston, Beulah Bondi, Guy Kibbee, Charles Coburn, John Carradine, Ann Rutherford

*Vivacious Lady* DIR George Stevens, starring Ginger Rogers, James Ellison, Charles Coburn

*The Shopworn Angel* DIR H C Potter, starring Margaret Sullavan, Walter Pidgeon, Hattie McDaniel

*You Can't Take it With You* DIR Frank Capra, starring Jean Arthur, Lionel Barrymore, Edward Arnold

### 1939
*Made for Each Other* DIR John Cromwell, starring Carole Lombard, Charles Coburn

*Ice Follies of 1939* DIR Reinhold Schunzel, starring Joan Crawford, Lew Ayres, Lewis Stone

*It's a Wonderful World* DIR W S Van Dyke II, starring Claudette Colbert, Guy Kibbee, Nat Pendleton

*Mr Smith Goes to Washington* DIR Frank Capra, starring Jean Arthur, Claude Rains, Edward Arnold

*Destry Rides Again* DIR George Marshall, starring Marlene Dietrich, Mischa Auer, Brian Donlevy

### 1940
*The Shop Around the Corner* DIR Ernst Lubitsch, starring Margaret Sullavan, Frank Morgan

*The Mortal Storm* DIR Frank Borzage, starring Margaret Sullavan, Robert Young, Frank Morgan

**Opposite:** James Stewart in his most important role – playing himself.

*No Time for Comedy* DIR William Keighley, starring Rosalind Russell, Genevieve Tobin, Charles Ruggles

*The Philadelphia Story* DIR George Cukor, starring Cary Grant, Katharine Hepburn

## 1941

*Come Live With Me* DIR Clarence Brown, starring Hedy Lamarr, Ian Hunter

*Pot O'Gold* British release title *The Golden Hour* DIR George Marshall, starring Paulette Goddard

*Ziegfeld Girl* DIR Robert Z Leonard, starring Lana Turner, Judy Garland, Hedy Lamarr, Jackie Cooper

## 1946

*It's A Wonderful Life* DIR Frank Capra, starring Donna Reed, Lionel Barrymore

## 1947

*Magic Town* DIR William A Wellman, starring Jane Wyman, Kent Smith

## 1948

*Call Northside 777* DIR Harry Hathaway, starring Lee J Cobb, Richard Conte

*On Our Merry Way* (also known as *A Miracle Can Happen*) DIR King Vidor, Leslie Fenton, starring Paulette Goddard, *Burgess Meredith, *Henry Fonda, Dorothy Lamour, Victor Moore, Fred MacMurray

*indicates some of the participants in the James Stewart episode

*Rope* DIR Alfred Hitchcock, starring Farley Granger, John Dall, Joan Chandler, Cedric Hardwicke, Constance Collier

*You Gotta Stay Happy* DIR H C Potter, starring Joan Fontaine, Eddie Albert, Roland Young

## 1949

*The Stratton Story* DIR Sam Wood, starring June Allyson, Frank Morgan, Agnes Moorehead

*Malaya* (British release title *East of the Rising Sun*) DIR Richard Thorpe, starring Spencer Tracy, Valentina Cortesa, Sidney Greenstreet, Lionel Barrymore, Gilbert Roland

## 1950

*Winchester 73* DIR Anthony Mann, starring Shelley Winters, Dan Duryea, Stephen McNally

*Broken Arrow* DIR Delmer Daves, starring Jeff Chandler, Debra Paget, Will Geer

*The Jackpot* DIR Walter Lang, starring Barbara Hale, James Gleason, Natalie Wood

*Harvey* DIR Henry Koster, starring Josephine Hull, Peggy Dow, Charles Drake

## 1951

*No Highway* (American release title *No Highway in the Sky*) DIR Henry Koster, starring Marlene Dietrich, Glynis Johns, Jack Hawkins, Janette Scott

## 1952

*The Greatest Show on Earth* DIR Cecil D DeMille, starring Betty Hutton, Cornel Wilde, Charlton Heston, Dorothy Lamour, Gloria Grahame

*Bend of the River* (British release title *Where the River Bends*) DIR Anthony Mann, starring Arthur Kennedy, Julia Adams, Rock Hudson, Lori Nelson

*Carbine Williams* DIR Richard Thorpe, starring Jean Hagen, Wendell Corey

*The Naked Spur* DIR Anthony Mann, starring Robert Ryan, Janet Leigh, Ralph Meeker, Millard Mitchell

## 1953

*Thunder Bay* DIR Anthony Mann, starring Joanne Dru, Gilbert Roland, Dan Duryea

*The Glenn Miller Story* DIR Anthony Mann, starring June Allyson, Henry 'Harry' Morgan, Charles Drake, George Tobias

*Below:* One of the loveliest scenes from the timeless *It's a Wonderful Life* (1946). Stewart escorts Donna Reed home from a dance, and they both became soaked after falling into a swimming pool. Although he doesn't quite realize it yet, Stewart is in love with his companion.

## 1954

*Rear Window* DIR Alfred Hitchcock, starring Grace Kelly, Wendell Corey, Thelma Ritter, Raymund Burr

## 1955

*The Far Country* DIR Anthony Mann, starring Ruth Roman, Corinne Calvert, Walter Brennan

*Strategic Air Command* DIR Anthony Mann, starring June Allyson, Barry Sullivan, Frank Lovejoy

*The Man From Laramie* DIR Anthony Mann, starring Arthur Kennedy, Donald Crisp, Cathy O'Donnell

## 1956

*The Man Who Knew Too Much* DIR Alfred Hitchcock, starring Doris Day, Bernard Miles, Brenda de Banzie

## 1957

*The Spirit of St Louis* DIR Billy Wilder, starring Murray Hamilton, Patricia Smith, Barlett Robinson

*Night Passage* DIR James Neilson, starring Audie Murphy, Dan Duryea, Dianne Foster, Elaine Stewart, Brandon de Wilde

## 1958

*Vertigo* DIR Alfred Hitchcock, starring Kim Novak, Barbara Bel Geddes, Tom Helmore, Henry Jones

*Bell, Book and Candle* DIR Richard Quine, starring Kim Novak, Jack Lemmon, Ernie Kovacs, Hermione Gingold, Elsa Lanchester

## 1959

*Anatomy of a Murder* DIR Otto Preminger, starring Lee Remick, Ben Gazarra, Joseph N Welch, George C Scott, Kathryn Grant, Eve Arden

*The FBI Story* DIR Mervyn Le Roy, starring Vera Miles, Murray Hamilton, Larry Pennell, Nick Adams

## 1960

*The Mountain Road* DIR Delbert Mann, starring Lisa Lu, Glenn Corbett, Henry 'Harry' Morgan, Frank Silvera

## 1961

*Two Rode Together* DIR John Ford, starring Richard Widmark, Shirley Jones, Linda Cristal

## 1962

*The Man Who Shot Liberty Valance* DIR John Ford, starring John Wayne, Vera Miles, Lee Marvin, Edmund O'Brien

*Mr Hobbs Takes a Vacation* DIR Henry Koster, starring Maureen O'Hara, Fabian, Lauri Peters, John Saxon

*How The West Was Won* DIR John Ford,

*Henry Hathaway, George Marshall, Richard Thorpe, starring Carroll Baker, Lee J Cobb, Henry Fonda, Carolyn Jones, *Karl Malden, Gregory Peck, George Peppard, Robert Preston, Debbie Reynolds, Eli Wallach, John Wayne, Richard Widmark, *Brigid Bazlen, *Walter Brennan, Raymond Massey, *Agnes Moorehead
(* indicates some of the participants in the James Steward episode 'The Rivers')

## 1963

*Take Her, She's Mine* DIR Henry Koster, starring Sandra Dee, Audrey Meadows, Robert Morley

## 1964

*Cheyenne Autumn* DIR John Ford, starring Richard Widmark, Carroll Baker, Karl Malden, *Arthur Kennedy, *Edward G Robinson, Patrick Wayne, *Elizabeth Allen, *John Carradine, *Judson Pratt
(*indicates participants in the James Stewart episode)

*Above:* Stewart suffers a bad attack of *Vertigo* in this famous still from the Hitchcock classic.

**Right:** Stewart took a cameo role in *Airport 77*. Like many veteran stars, he has found suitable roles hard to come by. This film also starred Olivia de Havilland, an old friend of Stewart's.

**Below:** Stewart holds the American Film Institute Life Achievement Award he received in February 1980.

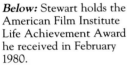

## 1965

*Dear Brigitte* DIR Henry Koster, starring Fabian, Glynis Johns, Cindy Carol, Billy Mumy

*Shenandoah* DIR Andrew V McLaglen, starring Doug McClure, Glenn Corbett, Patrick Wayne, Rosemary Forsyth, Katharine Ross

## 1968

*Bandolero* DIR Andrew V McLaglen, starring Dean Martin, Raquel Welch, George Kennedy, Andrew Prine, Will Geer

## 1970

*The Cheyenne Social Club* DIR Gene Kelly, starring Henry Fonda, Shirley Jones

## 1971

*Fool's Parade* (British release title *Dynamite Man from Glory Jail*) DIR Andrew V McLaglen, starring George Kennedy, Anne Baxter, Strother Martin, Kurt Russell

## 1976

*The Shootist* DIR Don Siegel, starring John Wayne, Lauren Bacall, Ron Howard, Richard Boone

## 1977

*Airport* DIR Jerry Jameson, starring Jack Lemmon, Lee Grant, Brenda Vaccarro, Joseph Cotton, Olivia de Havilland, Christopher Lee, George Kennedy

## 1978

*The Big Sleep* DIR Michael Winner, starring Joan Collins, Robert Mitchum, Sara Miles, Richard Boone, Candy Clark, John Mills, Oliver Reed, Harry Andrews, Colin Blakely, Richard Todd, Diana Quick

*The Magic of Lassie* DIR Don Chaffrey, starring Mickey Rooney, Stephanie Zimbalist, Alice Faye

## 1981

*The Green Horizon* DIR Susumu Hani, Simon Trevor, starring Philip Sayer, Eleonora Vallone, Hakuta Simba

# Index

Figures in *italics* refer to illustrations

## ACKNOWLEDGMENTS

The publisher would like to thank Martin Bristow, who designed this book; Sara Dunphy, for picture research; Pat Coward, who compiled the index; and Jessica Orebi Gann, the editor. We would also like to thank the following agencies and institutions for supplying illustrative material.

Bettmann Archive: pages 1, 6, 7, 9, 12, 13, 14, 21, 26, 27, 28 (bottom), 29 (bottom), 32 (bottom), 37 (bottom), 39, 41 (top), 43, 44, 49, 53, 55 (both), 56, 69 (bottom)

British Film Institute Stills, Posters and Designs: pages 58 (both), 59 (both), 67 (both), 70 (top left), 78 (top)

Brompton Photo Library: pages 2, 19, 33 (bottom), 34, 50, 51, 52, 54, 61, 62 (both), 63 (both), 65, 66 (top), 77

Courtesy of the National Film Archive Stills Library, London: pages 4, 45, 66 (bottom)

Photofest: page 75

Springer/Bettmann Film Archive: pages 5, 8, 15, 18 (both), 20, 22, 23, 24 (both), 25, 28 (top), 29 (top), 31, 32 (top), 33 (top), 35 (top), 36, 41 (top), 42, 57 (top), 64, 68, 69 (top), 72, 73

UPI/Bettmann: pages 10, 11, 16, 17, 30 (both), 35 (bottom), 37 (top), 38 (both), 40, 46 (both), 47, 48, 57 (bottom), 60, 70 (top right and bottom), 71 (both), 76, 78 (bottom)